An Introduction to Persian

Revised Fourth Edition
Key to Exercises

Wheeler M. Thackston

Ibex Publishers,
Bethesda, Maryland

An Introduction to Persian, Revised Fourth Edition
Key to Exercises
by Wheeler M. Thackston

Copyright © 2010 Ibex Publishers, Inc.

ISBN: 978-1-58814-054-8

Calligraphy on cover (16th-17th Centuries) courtesy of the Sackler Gallery of Art.

Manufactured in the United States of America

The paper used in this book meets the minimum requirements of the American National Standard for Information Services—Permanence of Paper for Printed Library Materials, ANSI Z39.48–1984

This is the key to exercises for *An Introduction to Persian, Revised Fourth Edition* (ISBN: 978-1-58814-055-5)

A CD set of the Persian sections of this book is also available. (ISBN-13: 978-1-58814-057-9).

Ibex Publishers, Inc.
Post Office Box 30087
Bethesda, Maryland 20824
Telephone: 301–718–8188
Facsimile: 301–907–8707
www.ibexpublishers.com

An Introduction to Persian
Revised 4th Edition
Key to Exercises

Exercise 1

(a) ۱ کشوری keshvár-i، کشورها keshvarhá، کشورهائی keshvarhá-i.

۲ کتابی ketáb-i، کتابها ketâbhá، کتابهائی ketâbhá-i.

۳ خانه‌ای khâné-i، خانه‌ها khânehá، خانه‌هائی khânehá-i.

۴ قلمی qalám-i، قلمها qalamhá، قلمهائی qalamhá-i.

۵ میزی míz-i، میزها mizhá، میزهائی mizhá-i.

۶ صندلی‌ای sandalí-i، صندلیها sandalihá، صندلیهائی sandalihá-i.

۷ کوهی kúh-i، کوهها kuhhá، کوههائی kuhhá-i.

۸ دری dár-i، درها darhá، درهائی darhá-i.

(b) 1. *miz-i boẕorg* a big table 2. *sandalihâ-i khub* some good chairs 3. *keshvar-i kuchek* a small country 4. *kuh-i boẕorg* a large country 5. *khânehâ-i qadimi* some old houses 6. *qalamhâ-i bad* some bad pens 7. *pâkkonhâ-i qadimi* some old erasers 8. *ketâb-i naw* a new book 9. *qalam-i khub* a good pen 10. *mizhâ-i naw* some new tables 11. *khân-i naw* a new house 12. *gach-i kuchek* a small piece of chalk 13. *keshvarhâ-i boẕorg* some large countries 14. *dar-i kuchek* a little door

(c) ۱ کوههائی کوچک. ۲ خانه‌هائی قدیمی. ۳ میزی قدیمی. ۴ صندلی‌ای نو. ۵ کشوری قدیمی. ۶ قلمی خوب. ۷ پاک‌کنی خوب. ۸ درهائی بزرگ. ۹ کتابهائی بد. ۱۰ گچهائی نو

Exercise 2

(الف) ۱ این، جوانی ایرانی است. ۲ آن، کوهی بزرگ است. ۳ آنها، بچه‌هائی بد بودند. ۴ تهران شهری بزرگ است. ۵ این، کشوری قدیمی است. ۶ آنها، میزهائی کوچک بودند. ۷ آنها، کتابهائی کوچک بودند. ۸ اینها، صندلیهائی نو بودند. ۹ آنها، پنجه‌هائی کوچکند. ۱۰ آمریکا کشوری بزرگ است.

(ب) ۱ بله، آن جوان ایرانی است. نخیر، آن جوان ایرانی نیست. ۲ بله، آن کشورها بسیار قدیمی‌اند. نخیر، آن کشورها بسیار قدیمی نیست (نیستند). ۳ بله، این بچه کوچک است. نخیر، این بچه کوچک نیست. ۴ بله، آن میزها خوبند. نخیر، آن میزها خوب نیست (نیستند). ۵ بله، آن صندلی کاملاً نو است. نخیر، آن صندلی کاملاً نو نیست. ۶ بله، این میز و صندلی خوبند. نخیر، این میز و صندلی خوب نیست (نیستند). ۷ بله، آن شهر در آمریکاست. نخیر، آن شهر در آمریکا نیست. ۸ بله، آن کوه خیلی کوچک است. نخیر، آن کوه خیلی کوچک نیست. ۹ بله، این کتابها قدیمی‌اند. نخیر، این کتابها قدیمی نیستند. ۱۰ بله، این گچ و پاک‌کن خوبند. نخیر، این گچ و پاک‌کن خوب نیستند.

(c) 1. *Ân kuh dar Âmrikâ nist.* That mountain is not in America. 2. *Ân ketâbhâ cherâ injâ nist?* Why are those books not here? 3. *Ân mizhâ bozorg nist vali khub-ast.* Those tables are not large, but they are good. 4. *Ân shahr cherâ bad-ast?* Why is that city bad? 5. *Âmrikâ keshvar-i bozorg-ast vali qadimi nist.* America is a large country, but it is not old. 6. *Ân irânihâ kojâ-budand?* Where were those Iranians? 7. *In miz o sandali bozorg o khub-and.* This table and chair are large and good. 8. *Irân keshvar-i qadimi-ast-o Tehrân shahr-i bozorg-ast dar Irân.* Iran is an old country, and Tehran is a large city in Iran. 9. *Ân javân irâni nist; âmrikâi-ast.* That youth is not Iranian; s/he is American. 10. *Inhâ ketâbhâ-i besyâr khub-and.* These are very good books.

(د) ۱. آن ایرانیها اینجا نیستند. ۲ آنها آنجا بودند. ۳ آن میز خیلی کوچک است. ۴ کتابها و قلمها در خانه است (اند). ۵ اینها صندلیهائی بسیار خوبند. ۶ آن شهر کجاست؟ ۷ تهران در ایران است. ۸ آن بچه‌ها ایرانی‌اند.

Exercise 3

(الف) ۱ دانشجوئی زرنگ > دانشجوی زرنگی ۲ پسرهائی خوشحال > پسرهای خوشحالی ۳ کشوری مشهور > کشورِ مشهوری ۴ خانه‌هائی خراب > خانه‌های خوابی ۵ مردی زرنگ > مردِ زرنگی ۶ بچه‌هائی بسیار زرنگ > بچه‌های بسیار زرنگی ۷ مردی خیلی تنبل > مردِ خیلی تنبلی ۸ کتابهائی نسبةً مفید > کتابهای نسبةً مفیدی ۹ دانشجوهائی خیلی خوب > دانشجوهای خیلی خوبی ۱۰ دانشگاهی کاملاً نو > دانشگاهِ کاملاً نوی

(ب) ۱ بله، آنها بچه‌اند. نخیر، آنها بچه نیستند. ۲ بله، این دانشگاه قدیمی است. نخیر،

4

این دانشگاه قدیمی نیست. ۳ بله، معلمهای خوبی بودند. نخیر، معلمهای خوبی نبودند. ۴ بله، تهران شهر خوبیست. نخیر، تهران شهر خوبی نیست. ۵ بله، اینها مردهای تنبلی اند. نخیر، اینها مردهای تنبلی نیستند. ۶ بله، آن بچهها ایرانی اند. نخیر، آن بچهها ایرانی نیستند. ۷ بله، آن دانشگاه مشهور در ایران است. نخیر، آن دانشگاه مشهور در ایران نیست. ۸ بله، این کتابها دربارهٔ ایران اند. نخیر، این کتابها دربارهٔ ایران نیست. ۹ بله، آن قلم کهنه مفید بود. نخیر، آن قلم کهنه مفید نبود. ۱۰ بله، آن پسرهای کوچک تنبل زرنگند. نخیر، آن پسرهای کوچک تنبل زرنگ نیستند.

(ج) ۱ این جوان، ایرانی است. ۲ آن، شهر بزرگیست. ۳ آن بچهها، خوبند. ۴ آنها، پنجرههای کوچکی اند. ۵ آن میزها، کوچک بودند. ۶ آن، کتاب قدیمیای بود. ۷ این، صندلی نوی بود. ۸ این کشور، قدیمی است. ۹ اینها، کشورهای بزرگی اند. ۱۰ آنها، دانشجوهای خوبی اند.

(d) 1. *Tehrân shahr-i-st bozorg-o nesbatan qadimi.* Tehran is a large and relatively old city. 2. *Ân khânehâ-ye kohne kharâb-budand.* Those old houses were ruined. 3. *Ânhâ pesar nistand; mard-and.* They are not boys; they are men. 4. *In pesar-e tambal-i nist.* This is not a lazy boy. 5. *Ân dâneshju-ye zerang dar dâneshgâh nist.* That clever student is not in the university. 6. *Cherâ dar in shahr ketâb-e khub-i nist?* Why is there not a good book in this city? 7. *Dar ân dâneshgâhhâ dâneshjuhâ tambal nistand.* In those universities the students are not lazy. 8. *Ân ketâb injâ nist. Kojâ-st?* That book is not here. Where is it? 9. *In ketâbhâ-ye qadimi darbâre-ye Irân-and?* Are these old books about Iran? 10. *Ân mard-i-st besyâr mashhur dar Irân.* He is a very well-known man in Iran.

(هـ) ۱ آن قلم کهنه خراب است. ۲ (آن) دانشجو نیست. ۳ (آنها) دانشجوهای خوبی اند. ۴ (آن) در تهران نیست ولی خوشحال است. ۵ آن خانههای قدیمی بزرگ کاملاً خوب است (اند). ۶ این، کشور نسبةً قدیمیایست. ۷ (آنها) پسرهای زرنگی اند. ۸ آن مرد کجاست؟ ۹ (آنها) در آن شهر قدیمی نبودند. ۱۰ بچهها آنجا نبودند.

Exercise 4

(الف) ۱ من همیشه خوشحالم. ۲ آنها تنبلند. ۳ شما بچه نیستید. ۴ تو بچهای. ۵ ما پزشک نیستیم. ۶ شما معلمید؟ ۷ این آقا کیست؟ ۸ آن چیست؟ ۹ ما کجائیم؟ ۱۰ آن جعبه بزرگ است. ۱۱ این خانمها مهربانند؟ ۱۲ تو بچهٔ خوبیای؟ ۱۳ شما پزشکید؟ ۱۴ من ایرانی ام.

(ب) ۱ ما دانشجوهای خوبی ایم. ۲ شما پزشک مشهوری اید. شما پزشکهای مشهوری اید. ۳ شما دانشجو اید؟ ۴ او مرد خوشحالیست. ۵ آنها بچههای زرنگی بودند. ۶ این کتابها نسبةً مفید بود. ۷ آن مردها پزشکهای بزرگی اند در ایران. ۸ من دانشجو ام در دانشگاه تهران. ۹ آن بچهایست زرنگ ولی تنبل. ۱۰ این جوانها دانشجو بودند.

(ج) ۱ آن مرد مهربان کیست؟ ۲ در آن جعبهٔ سیاه بزرگ چیست؟ ۳ چرا خوشحال نیستید؟ ۴ پزشک نیستم، معلمم در این شهر. ۵ آن زن کیست؟ ۶ آن خانم علیزاده نیست؟ ۷ من در این دانشگاه دانشجو ام (من دانشجو ام در این دانشگاه).

Exercise 5

(الف) ۱ بله، این بچه پسر من است. نخیر، این بچه پسر من نیست. ۲ بله، من دخترِ او هستم. نخیر من دخترِ او نیستم. ۳ بله، او مادرِ علی است. نخیر، او مادرِ علی نیست. ۴ بله، شما پدرِ آن بچهاید. نخیر، شما پدرِ آن بچه نیستید. ۵ بله، کتابهای من اینها هستند. نخیر، کتابهای من اینها نیستند. ۶ بله، اینها کتابهای شما هستند. نخیر، اینها کتابهای شما نیستند. ۷ بله، راه تهران از اینجاست. نخیر، راه تهران از اینجا نیست. ۸ بله، تهران شهر بزرگ ایران است. نخیر، تهران شهر بزرگ ایران نیست. ۹ بله، او پدرِ خانم علیزاده است. نخیر، او پدرِ خانم علیزاده نیست.

(ب) ۱ کتابهای جدید ما در خانهٔ شما هستند. ۲ بله، خانهٔ من به اینجا خیلی نزدیک است. نخیر، خانهٔ من از اینجا دور است. ۳ کشور من آمریکاست. ۴ بله، آن دخترها با من بودند. ۵ نخیر، کتاب پسر کوچک او در خانه نیست. ۶ بله، تهران از اینجا خیلی دور است. ۷ بله، خانهٔ شما نزدیک خانهٔ من است. نخیر، خانهٔ شما نزدیک خانهٔ من نیست. ۸ اسم من علی است. ۹ امروز در تهران بودند. ۱۰ این برای شماست.

(ج) ۱ کتاب جدید علی > یکی از کتابهای جدید علی. ۲ خانهٔ آقای علیزاده > یکی از خانههای آقای علیزاده. ۳ شهر ایران > یکی از شهرهای ایران. ۴ بچهٔ آن زن > یکی از بچههای آن زن. ۵ پسر مادر من > یکی از پسرهای مادر من. ۶ راهِ دورِ آن کشور > یکی از

6

راههای دورِ آن کشور. ۷ دانشجوی دانشگاه > یکی از دانشجوهای دانشگاه. ۸ خانهٔ این شهر > یکی از خانههای این شهر

(d) 1. *Khâne-ye jadid-e mâdar-o pedar-e shomâ kojâ-st?* Where is your mother and father's new house? 2. *Emruz ân mard-e mehrbân-i irâni dar ân shahr bud.* That kind Iranian man was in that city today. 3. *Shahr-e Tehrân az Âmrikâ khayli dur-ast.* The city of Tehran is very far from America. 4. *Khânom-e Alizâde, shomâ mâdar-e ân dokhtar-e kuchek hastid?* Ms Alizadeh, are you that little girl's mother? 5. *Khâne-ye ânhâ kojâ-ye Tehrân bud?* Whereabouts in Tehran is their house? 6. *Yek-i az in ketâbhâ-ye naw barâ-ye Ali-ast.* One of these new books is for Ali.

(هـ) ۱ اسمِ آن پسرِ کوچک چیست؟ ۲ این برای زنِ شماست؟ ۳ نخیر، برای او نیست، برای دخترِ کوچکِ من است. ۴ آن کتابِ نوِ شما دربارهٔ چیست؟ ۵ ما ایرانی نیستیم، آمریکائی هستیم. ۶ خانهٔ شما از شهر دور نیست.

Review I

(b) 1. *In âqâ mo'allem-ast.* This gentleman is a teacher. 2. *Ân khânom mo'allem-i-st besyâr mehrbân.* That lady is a very kind teacher. 3. *Dokhtar-e kuchek-e shomâ hamishe khoshhâl bud.* Your little girl was always happy. 4. *Âqâ, dar ân ja'be-ye bozorg chist?* Sir, what's in that big box? 5. *Dâneshjuhâ-ye dânesgâh kojâ-and?* Where are the university students? 6. *In qalam-e kohne kâmelan kharâb-ast.* This old pen is perfectly good. 7. *Ishân zanhâ-ye nesbatan zerang-i-and.* They are relatively clever women. 8. *Pedar-e u dar yek-i az shahrhâ-ye Irân pezeshk bud.* His father was a physician in one of the cities of Iran. 9. *Mo'allem-e ân javân-e zerang-e irâni shomâ-id?* Are you the teacher of that clever Iranian young person? 10. *Inhâ sandalihâ-ye khub-i nist.* These are not good chairs.

(ج) ۱ اسمِ او چه بود؟ ۲ خانهٔ ما نسبةً نزدیکِ تهران است. ۳ ایران کشوریست بزرگ و بسیار قدیمی. ۴ کتابها و قلمهای من کجاست (کجا اند)؟ ۵ پنجرههای این خانه بسیار کوچک است (اند). ۶ شما دانشجو نیستید؟ ۷ آن کتاب دربارهٔ چه بود؟ ۸ قلمِ نوِ شما سبز نیست؟ ۹ نخیر، سبز نیست، سیاه است. ۱۰ در این شهر خانههای بسیار کوچکی هست.

Exercise 6

(الف) ۱ ما دیدیم. ۲ آنها آوردند. ۳ ایشان چه گرفتند؟ ۴ او نشنید. ۵ من آوردم. ۶ تو

این‌را خواستی. ۷ شما مرا دیدید. ۸ ما آن‌را گرفتیم. ۹ آن‌را اینها خواستند. ۱۰ من آنجا بودم. ۱۱ ما ایران‌را دیدیم. ۱۲ این صندلی‌را کی آورد؟ ۱۳ من قلم شمارا گرفتم. ۱۴ تو آن‌هارا به او دادی. ۱۵ شما شنیدید؟ ۱۶ دوستهای ایشان اینهارا برای ما آوردند. ۱۷ او در آن شهر نبود. ۱۸ دانشجوها کتابهارا گرفتند.

(ب) ۱ چرا، خوب است. ۲ چرا خواستم. ۳ چرا، بد بود. ۴ چرا، آوردم. ۵ چرا، شمارا دیدم. ۶ چرا، اینجا بودند. ۷ چرا، آن چیزهارا به علی داد. ۷ چرا، در خانهٔ دوست من هستند. ۸ چرا، از اینجا دور است. ۹ چرا، شنیدم.

(c) 1. *Dusthâ-ye mâ-râ nadidand.* They did not see our friends. 2. *Ân qalam-e digar-râ khâst.* He wanted that other pen. 3. *Ketâb-e marâ be u dâdi?* Did you give my book to him? 4. *Ânhâ-râ shenidam.* I heard them. 5. *Ân chizhâ-râ cherâ nagereftid?* Why didn't you take those things? 6. *Ketâbhâ-râ âvordim.* We brought the books. 7. *Mâdar-o pedar-e shomâ-râ dar khâne-ye Âqâ-ye Ja'fari didam.* I saw your mother and father in Mr. Ja'fari's house. 8. *Inhâ-râ nakhâstim.* We did not want these. 9. *Ân-râ shenidid?* Did you hear that? 10. *Inha-râ ki âvord?* Who brought these?

(د) ۱ آن‌را نشنیدید؟ چرا، شنیدم. ۲ دیروز دوست من از این کتابهارا به کتابخانه آورد. ۳ این چیزهارا کی خواست؟ ۴ قلمهارا به دوستهای ما دادند. ۵ دیروز مادر مریم‌را ندیدم. ۶ ماهم آن‌هارا روی میز دیدیم. ۷ چیزی نیاوردم. ۸ آن‌هارا به دوست من دادند. ۹ دیروز شمارا در کتابخانه دیدم. ۱۰ این کتاب‌را نخواستید؟ چرا، خواستم.

Exercise 7

(الف) ۱ دوست من نامه مینوشت. ۲ چرا کار ما پیش نمیرفت؟ ۳ مادر و پدر من در این خانه زندگی میکردند. ۴ من از شهر به خانه برمیگشتم. ۵ آن کتابهارا ما میخواندیم. ۶ علی و مریم به مدرسه میرفتند. ۷ من آن چیزهارا برمیداشتم. ۸ شما از مدرسه میآمدید. ۹ دوستهای من خیلی درس میخواندند. ۱۰ او کتاب خوبی داشت.

(ب) ۱ من هم یک نامه‌ای نوشته‌ام. ۲ قلم مرا کی برداشته‌است. ۳ شما هم مدرسه رفته‌اید؟ ۴ او هم کتابی نوشته است. ۵ در این خانه کی زندگی کرده است؟ ۶ کار شما خیلی پیش رفته است. ۷ شما چرا اینهارا آورده‌اید؟ ۸ ما فارسی خوانده‌ایم. ۹ من خیلی کتاب خوانده‌ام.

۱۰ آنها صدای شمارا نشنیده‌اند.

(ج) ۱ امروز کی آمده است؟ ۲ فارسی میخواندم. ۳ روزنامه‌ها روی میز بوده اند. ۴ خیلی کتاب میخواندم. ۵ از مدرسه برنگشته‌اند. ۶ امروز کار نکرده‌اید. ۷ دیروز نامه مینوشتیم. ۸ آنرا به شما نداده‌اند؟ ۹ کتابخانه خیلی کتاب داشت. ۱۰ مدرسه نرفته است، خیلی کوچک است.

Exercise 8

(الف) ۱ به به، آن شهر چه آرام بود! ۲ به به، چه دخترهای خوبی اند! ۳ وای، آن درس چه سخت بود! ۴ وای، آن چه زمستان سردی بود! ۵ وای، این تابستان چه گرم است! ۶ وای، چه کارِ سختی بود! ۷ به به، چه مدرسهٔ قدیمی‌ایست! ۸ وای، امروز چه روزِ سردیست! ۹ وای، دیروز چه گرم بود! ۱۰ به به، اینها چه کتابهای آسانی اند!

(ب) ۱ در ایران چه شهرهائی دیدید؟ ۲ در آمریکا چه کار میکردید؟ ۳ دیروز چه کاری کردند؟ ۴ در خانهٔ علی چه نامه‌ای خواندید؟ ۵ امروز چه روزنامه‌ای خوانده‌اید؟ ۶ از آنجا چه کتابهائی برداشتند؟ ۷ آن خانم چه چیزهائی میخواست؟ ۸ مریم چه چیزهائی به شما داده است؟

(ج) ۱ تهران و اصفهان‌را دیده‌ام. ۲ دیروز آن کتابِ فارسی‌را خواندند. ۳ از روی میز علی این نامه‌را برداشتم. ۴ آن مرد این چیزرا گرفته است. ۵ مریم در دانشگاه تهران درس خوانده است. ۶ ما دانشجوهای دانشگاهِ تهرانیم. ۷ من پدرِ آن دخترم. ۸ به کتابخانهٔ دانشگاه رفتند.

(د) ۱ این خانه از آن خانه‌های دیگر آرامتر است. ۲ امروز از دیروز گرمتر است. ۳ زمستان از تابستان سردتر است. ۴ این کار از آن کار سختتر است. ۵ من از شما بیشتر درس خواندم. ۶ روزنامه‌های تهران از آن دیگرها بهترند. ۸ ما از شما زودتر آمدیم. ۹ آنها از من زودتر برگشتند. ۱۰ او از من بیشتر نامه نوشت.

(ه) ۱ بهترین کتابها اینها اند. کتابهای بهتر از همه اینها اند. ۲ بلندترین مرد آن است. مردِ از همه بلندتر آن است. ۳ سختترین کار اینست. کارِ سختتر از همه اینست. ۳ گرمترین روز

9

دیروز بود. روزِ گرمتر از همه دیروز بود. ۵ سردترین روز امروز است. روزِ از همه سردتر امروز است. ۶ زرنگترین دانشجوها اینها اند. دانشجوهای زرنگتر از همه اینها اند. ۷ مشهورترین مرد علی است. مردِ مشهورتر از همه علی است. ۸ آسانترین درس این است. درسِ آسانتر از همه این است. ۹ کوتاهترین پسر این است. پسرِ کوتاهتر از همه این است. ۱۰ بهتردین پزشک آن آقاست. پزشکِ بهتر از همه آن آقاست.

Exercise 9

(الف) ۱ بله، آن باغ بزرگ مال ماست. ۲ این جعبهٔ سیاه مال اوست. ۳ چرا، من مال این ده هستم. ۴ این دهات مال شهر اصفهان‌اند. ۵ چرا، آن قلم مال مریم است. ۶ بله، میدانستم این مال کجاست. ۷ از آنها، این یکی بیشتر بود. ۸ این مال آنهاست.

(b) 1. *Ân irâniân kojâ zendegi-mikardand?* Where did those Iranians used to live? 2. *In dâneshjuyân bishtar dars-khândeand tâ ânân.* These students have studied more than those. 3. *Dar entekhâbât-e emsâl ki entekhâb shode-ast?* Who was elected in this year's elections? 4. *Ânân-râ har ruz midideam vali emruz nayâmadeand.* I have been seeing them every day, but they haven't come today. 5. *Pedar-e Ali-o Maryam be shahr-e bozorg rafte-o barnagashte-ast.* Ali and Maryam's father has gone to the big city and not returned. 6. *Chera ânhâ-râ entekhâb-kardand?* Why did they select them? 7. *Nemidânestam ke in mâl-e Ali-ast yâ mâl-e pedar-e shomâ.* I didn't know whether this belonged to Ali or to your father. 8. *Dishab dar bâq-e bozorg-i mive-ye khoshmaze-i mikhordim.* Last night we were eating delicious fruit in a large garden. 9. *Chêrâ bolandtar nagoftid? Sedâ-ye shomâ-râ nashenidam.* Why didn't you say it louder? I didn't hear you. 10. *Bachchehâ-ye ân deh hame-ye mivehâ-ye bâq-e shomâ-râ khordeand.* The children of that village have eaten all the fruit of your garden.

(ج) ۱ شما در شهرِ کوچکی بزرگ شدید؟ ۲ در روزهای سردِ زمستان به مدرسه میرفتیم. ۳ دیروز علی و پدر اورا کجا دیدید؟ ۴ برای شما کدام درس از همه آسانتر بود؟ ۵ در آنجا چه دوستهای خوبی داشتیم! ۶ پزشک‌را دیده‌اید؟ ۷ زندگانی بسیار سختی داشته‌ام! ۸ در کتابخانهٔ دانشگاه کتاب از همه بهتررا پیدا کردیم. کتاب از همه بهتر کتابخانهٔ دانشگاه‌را پیدا کردیم. ۹ خانهٔ شما بمراتب از خانهٔ من آرامتر است. ۱۰ پارسال دانشجوها از امسال بیشتر درس خواندند (پارسال دانشجوها بیشتر درس خواندند تا امسال).

(الف) ۱ بزرگ میشوند. ۲ آنرا پیدا میکنم. ۳ آنرا نمیداند. ۴ اینهارا کی میخرد؟ ۵ میوه میخورید؟ ۶ ما میگوئیم. ۷ علی نمیآید. ۸ تو چه داری؟ ۹ آنان برنمیگردند. ۱۰ کجا میروید؟ ۱۱ خیلی درس میخوانیم. ۱۲ اینرا تو مینویسی. ۱۳ هیچ چیزی نمیآورم. ۱۴ اینهارا نمیخواهند. ۱۵ چه میدهند؟ ۱۶ مارا نمیبینید. ۱۷ آنرا میشنوی؟ ۱۸ شمارا نمیشناسند. ۱۹ آنرا میگیریم. ۲۰ کی گوش میکند؟ ۲۱ کجا میمانند؟ ۲۲ آنهارا نمیبرم. ۲۳ به این سؤال جواب میدهید. ۲۴ فارسی حرف میزند. ۲۵ آنرا روی میز میگذارم. ۲۶ نمیفهمیم. ۲۷ گوش نمیکنم. ۲۸ ایشان چطورند؟ ۲۹ علیرا میزند. ۳۰ اینهارا کی میبرد؟

(b) 1. *Qabl az fardâ shab hame-ye inhâ-râ be khâne-ye u mibarim.* We'll carry these things to his house before tomorrow night. 2. *Pedar-e ân dokhtarân-râ mishenâsam.* I know those girls' father. 3. *Sedâ-ye marâ khub mishenavid? Gush nemikonid?* Do you hear my voice well? Are you listening? 4. *In mive-ye khoshmaze-râ ru-ye miz migozâram.* I'll put this delicious fruit on the table. 5. *Nemiguyam ke bad bud vali khub-ham nabud.* I don't say it was bad, but it wasn't good either. 6. *Be so'âl-e man javâb-nemidehand.* They won't answer my question. 7. *Ba'd az ân, yek sâl mândim dar ân keshvar.* After that, we stayed in that country for one year. 8. *Harfhâ-ye shomâ-râ khub mifahmam.* I understand well what you say. 9. *Ân-râ nemikhâham; in-râ mikhâham.* I don't want that one; I want this one. 10. *Khayli kâr-mikonim. Cherâ kâr-e ma bish az pish sakht mishavad?* We work a lot. Why is our work getting harder than ever?

(ج) ۱ شما سؤال میکنید و من جواب میدهم. ۲ اسم اورا نمیدانید؟ ۳ همیشه با او فارسی حرف میزنیم. ۴ کدام یکیرا میخرید؟ ۵ از شهر کی برمیگردند؟ ۶ هر روز به مدرسه میرویم و آنجا میخوانیم و مینویسیم. ۷ علی این چیزهارا به خانهٔ مریم میبرد. ۸ مادر و پدر مرا میشناسید؟ ۹ حرفهای اورا نمیفهمم. ۱۰ فردا همه چیزرا نزدیک در میگذاریم و آنها میبرند.

Review II

(b) 1. *Dishab man az hamishe bishtar dars-khândam.* Last night I studied more than ever. 2. *Ârâmtarin jâ-ye in shahr kojâ-st?* Where is the quietest place in this city? 3. *Ânhâ che khub fârsi harf-mizanand!* How well they speak Persian! 4. *Ruz-e az hame garmtar-e in tâbestan diruz bud.* Yesterday was the warmest day of this summer. 5. *Shenideam ke ân shahr yek-i az sardtarin shahrhâ-ye Irân-ast.* I have heard that that city is one of the coldest cities in Iran. 6. *Goftand ke ba'd az in, dâneshjuyân barnemigardand.* They said that after this the students will not return. 7. *Kodâm yek-i az inhâ-râ bishtar mikhâhid?* Which one of these do you want more? 8. *Che harfhâ-ye khub-i mizanid!* What good things you say! 9. *In nâme-râ dar ketâbkhâne-ye dânesgâh paydâ-kardeam.* I have found this letter in the university library. 10. *Bachchehâ khoshmazetarin mivehâ-râ az bâq bardâshtand-o raftand.* The children picked up the most delicious fruits from the garden and left.

(ج) ۱. پارسال کار سخت‌تر بود تا امسال. ۲ چرا بهترین میوه‌های باغ‌را برای ما انتخاب نکردند؟ ۳ هم انگیسی هم فارسی میخواند؟ ۴ پسرها و دخترهای او به کدام مدرسه میروند؟ ۵ همهٔ جوابهای شما خوب بود. ۶ این چیزها‌را برای من از کی میخرید؟ ۷ من اینها میبرم و شما انهارا (میبرید). ۸ همیشه کتابهایشان‌را روی میز میگذارند. ۹ هیچ چیزی نفهمیدند. ۱۰ بهترین دانشجوی این دانشگاه کیست؟

Exercise 11

(الف) ۱ قلمهایتان‌را ندید. ۲ صدایشان‌را نشنیده‌ایم. ۳ کتابش‌را میخواستی. ۴ کتابهای نومرا نخوانده‌اند. ۵ خانه‌اش‌را دیده‌ام. ۶ میز کهنه‌مان‌را علی می‌آورد. ۷ چیزهایش‌را از روی میز برمیدارم. ۸ نامهٔ مهمتان‌را میخواند. ۹ نامه‌هایتان‌را روی میز گذاشته‌ام. ۱۰ چایمان‌را میخورند.

(b) 1. *Cherâ kâr-e khodesh-râ nemikonad?* Why doesn't he do your own work? (Why doesn't he mind his own business?) 2. *In dar-râ ki bâz-kardeast? Man diruz bástamesh.* Who has opened this door? I shut it yesterday. 3. *So'âlesh-râ khub fahmidim vali u javâbemân-râ nashenid.* We understood his question well, but he didn't hear our answer. 4. *Hâlâ bâ barâdar-o khâharam chây mikhoram.* I'm drinking tea with my brother and sister now. 5. *Ba'd az kâr chây mikhorid yâ qahve?* After work do you drink tea, or coffee? 6. *In kârhâ az ânhâ khayli mohemmtar-ast.* These things are much more important than those. 7. *Mardom cherâ u-râ entekhâb-kardeand?* Why did the people elect (select, choose) him? 8. *Bâ inhame, hichvaqt be ânjâ nemiresim.* With all (stuff) this we'll never get there. 9. *Hamishe bâ hamin qalam-e qadimi nâmehâyetân-râ minevisid?* Do you always write your letters with this same old pen? 10. *Barâdarânetân-râ didam vali nashenâkhtameshân.* I saw your brothers, but I didn't recognize them.

(ج) ۱ دوستانم در ده کوچکی نزدیک تهران زندگی میکنند. ۲ به خانهٔ قدیمیشان برمیگردند چونکه خانهٔ دیگررا فروخته‌اند. ۳ دیروز یکی از دانشجویانتان‌را در کتابخانه دیدیم. ۴ یکی

12

از پنجره‌هارا می‌بندد. ۵ آنهمه‌را به کجا می‌برید؟ ۶ هیچوقت خانهٔ خودرا به آنها نمی‌فروشم.
۷ کتاب خیلی مهمی(را) برای کلاس فردا می‌خوانم. ۸ چرا از پنجره نگاه می‌کنید؟ چه
می‌بینید؟ ۹ چای می‌خورید یا قهوه؟ قهوه می‌خورم، هیچوقت چای نمی‌خورم. ۱۰ به چه نگاه
می‌کنید؟ به این کتابهای فارسی نگاه می‌کنم.

Exercise 12

(الف) ۱۵۷ صد و پنجاه و هفت، ۵,۲ پنج و دو دهم، ۳۸۹۲ سه هزار و هشتصد و نود و دو،
۶,۲۵ شش و ربع، ۶۶ شصت و شش، ۷,۷۵ هفت و سه ربع، ۱۹۸۳ هزار و نهصد و هشتاد
و سه، ۲۴۲ دویست و چهل و دو، ۱۳۶۱ هزار و سیصد و شصت و یک، ۵۱۱ پانصد و
یازده، ۴۷۰۲۱ چهل و هفت هزار و بیست و یک، ۹۰۱ نهصد و یک

(b) 1. *Sâ'at yek bist-o-chahârom-e shabâneruz-ast.* An hour is one twenty-fourth
of a day. 2. *Sânie yek shastom-e daqiqe-ast-o dar har sâ'st shast daqiqe hast.* A
second is one sixtieth of a minute, and there are sixty minutes in every hour. 3.
In shahr az ân shahr-e digar haftsad kilometr dur-ast. This city is seven hundred
kilometers distant from that other city. 4. *Do daqiqe sad-o-bist sânie-ast-o do
shabâneruz chehel-o-hast sâ'at-ast.* Two minutes are a hundred and twenty
seconds, and two days are forty-eight hours. 5. *Emruz-o fardâ se tâ dars mikhânim.*
Today and tomorrow we will study three lessons. 6. *In keshvar vishtar az devist tâ
ruznâme dârad.* This country has more than two hundred newspapers. 7. *Mâ
davâzdah sâl madrase-rafteim.* We have gone to school for twelve years. 8.
Aqallan ruz-i chahâr daf'e anhâ-râ mibinam. I see them at least four times a day. 9.
Yek sâ'at-o nim dar ânjâ mândim. We stayed there for an hour and a half. 10. *Dar
har mâh chahâr hafte hast-o dar har sâl davâzdah mâh.* There are four weeks in
every month, and twelve months in every year.

(ج) ۱ نیم ساعت میمانند یا سه ربع ساعت؟ ۲ در این ماه سی و یک روز هست. ۳ دو تا
برادر و سه تا خواهر دارم. ۴ درس اول آسان بود، ولی درس دوم سختتر بود. ۵ شش ساعت
کار کردیم. ۶ هفتهٔ گذشتهٔ آن پنج تا کتاب‌را خواندم. ۷ همان سه تا صندلی سبزرا می‌خواهید؟
۸ تقریباً ساعت سه و نیم است (در حدود ساعت سه و نیم است). ۹ تابستان و زمستان
هرکدام سه ماه دارد. ۱۰ اقلا امروز آن پنجره‌را چهار دفعه بسته‌ام.

13

(الف) ۱ درس آسانی که خواندیم درس سوم بود. ۲ آن ساختمانهای بلندی که دیدهاند در شهر تهران بودند. ۳ آن تابستانی که گرم بود در تهران بودیم. ۴ پولی که داده بودم کم بود. ۵ آن زمستانی که زیاد سرد نبود کجا بودید؟ ۶ همسایگانی که رفتند برنگشتهاند. ۷ آن مردانی که بسیار پول دارند ایرانی اند. ۸ نامهای که زود رسید از برادرم است. ۹ آن کسانی که نیآمدند دوستان منند. ۱۰ آن دختر خوشگلی را که برگشته است دیدید؟

(ب) ۱ آن زانسجوئی که دیروز اینجا بوده است کجاست؟ ۲ آن زنی که میشناسیم میوه میخرید. ۳ پولی که از ما گرفتند زیاد نبود. ۴ آن روزی که شما میئید ما به شیراز میرویم. ۵ فاصلهای که شیراز با اصفهان دارد زیاد نیست. ۶ اطاقی که در آن زندگی میکردم بزرگ نبود. ۷ همسایهمان که به شیراز رفته است کی برمیگردد؟ ۸ آن چیزهائی را که روی میز گذاشتهام فراموش نمیکنم. ۹ آن روزی که شما از آن تعریف میکنید کی بود؟ ۱۰ آن ایرانیانی که با آنها بودیم زرنگند.

(ج) ۱ هنوز دررا باز نکرده بودم که اورا دیدم. ۲ خانهای که در آن زندگی میکردیم از شهر دور بود. ۳ اسم کسی را که دیروز با شما اینجا بود فراموش کردهام. ۴ پولی که از آنها گرفتید کجاست؟ ۵ ساعتی را که اینجا بود به جای دیگری بردید؟ ۶ ماه گذشته در شهری بود که با اینجا دویست کیلومتر فاصله دارد. ۷ نامهای را که روی میز گذاشتم فراموش کردم. ۸ ساختمانی که دوستان شما در آن زندگی میکنند از اینجا دور است؟ ۹ تقریباً پنج کیلومتر است از مدرسهای که به آن میرفتید. ۱۰ همهٔ چیزهائی را که به من دادید شمردم. جمعاً شانزده تا بود.

(الف) ۱ از او خواهد ترسید. ۲ در انتخابات کی انتخاب خواهد شد؟ ۳ هیچوفت بزرگ نخواهی شد! ۴ برای ایشان تعریف خواهم کرد. ۵ خواهند دانست. ۶ فراموش خواهید کرد. ۷ آنرا به شما نشان نخواهم داد. ۸ آنرا من خواهم گفت. ۹ سه هفته در آنجا خواهند گذراند. ۱۰ آنرا نخواهم خورد. ۱۱ آنهارا خواهیم خرید. ۱۲ او خواهد مرد. ۱۳ هفتهٔ آینده خواید رسید. ۱۴ گران خواهند خرید.

(ب) ۱ دو سال در آن گشور بودیم. ۲ پارسال سه دفعه به تهران رفتند. ۳ چهار کیلو میوه میخواهیم. ۴ اینرا ده دلار خریدم. ۵ امروز پنجشنبه است. ۶ در یک شبانه‌روز بیست و چهار ساعت هست. ۷ ماه گذشته سی روز داشت. ۸ من بیست و پنج سال دارم. ۹ این درس چهاردهم این کتاب است. ۱۰ در خانه‌مان شش تا اطاق هست.

(c) 1. *Qaymat-i-ke barâ-ye inhâ dâdi ziâd nabud.* The price you paid for these wasn't too much. 2. *Midânid keshvarhâ-ye hamsâye-ye Irân chistand?* Do you know what the countries neighboring Iran are? 3. *Ânhâ-râ anzântar mikhâham.* I want those cheaper. 4. *Hatman midânid in kist.* You must know who this is. 5. *Pul-i-ke az u gerefteam kam-ast.* The money I got from him is too little. 6. *Ân sâkhtemân-e bozorg-i-ke mibinid devist tâ otâq bishtar dârad.* That large building you see has more than two hundred rooms. 7. *Fâsele-i-ke ân dehât bâ shahr dârad ziâd nist.* The distance between those villages and the city is not great. 8. *Az kodâm hamsâyetân ta'rif-mikardid?* Which neighbor of yours were you talking about? 9. *In nemune-ash-ast. Khodesh nist.* This is an example of it, not the thing itself. 10. *Hanuz az ânjâ barnagashte-bud ke khâharesh mord.* Scarcely had he returned from there when his sister died.

(د) ۱ دوازده سال بیشتر ندارد. ۲ سومین خانه‌ای که می‌بینید مال ماست. ۳ هنوز به باغ نرسیده بودیم که همسایه‌هایشان آمدند. ۴ آنقدر کار میکند که میدانم که نمیرود. ۵ این چیزها را چطور ایقدر ارزان میخرید؟ ۶ چند تا نمونهٔ کارش‌را (نمونه‌هائی چند از کارش‌را) به شما نشان میدهد. ۷ سال آینده سه هفته در فرانسه میگذرانیم. ۸ ماه گذشته دو کیلوگرم قهوهٔ خیلی خوب خریدیم. ۹ ایرانیان روزی چند دفعه چای میخورند و تقریبا هیچوقت قهوه نمی‌خورند. ۱۰ همهٔ دانشجویانی‌را که در کلاسهایتان اند میشناسید؟

Exercise 15

(الف) ۱ بیرون برو (بروید). ۲ سه روز بیشتر نمان (نمانید)! ۳ اینرا داشته باش (داشته باشید). ۴ کتابش‌را همانجا بگذار (بگذارید). ۵ یکچند روزی همینجا بگذران (بگذرانید). ۶ حرفهای مرا گوش کن (گوش کنید). ۷ اینها را ارزان نفروش (نفروشید). ۸ خودرا بشناس (بشناسید). ۹ همیشه فارسی صحبت کن (صحبت کنید). ۱۰ زیاد سؤال نکن (سؤال نکنید). ۱۱ اینرا گم نکن (گم نکنید). ۱۲ حرفهایش‌را بفهم (بفهمید). ۱۳ آنها را بمن نشان بده (نشان بدهید). ۱۴ به سؤالم جواب بده (جواب بدهید). ۱۵ برو، گم شو (بروید، گم شوید). ۱۶ با ما حرف بزن (حرف بزنید). ۱۷ اینها را بیرون ببر (ببرید).

15

(b) 1. *Ân pirmardân-i-ke darbâre-shân sohbat-mikardim, zanhâ-yeshân kojâ-and?* Where are the wives of those old men about whom we were speaking? 2. *Ettefâqan dustam az hamân mâjarâ barâ-ye mâ ta'rif-mikard.* By chance my friend was telling us about the same adventure. 3. *Hatman ânhâ-râ qablan dideid.* You must have seen them before. 4. *Âqajân, inqadr kâr-nakonid. Mariz-mishavid!* Sir, don't work so much. You'll get sick! 5. *In naw' so'âl-râ dust-nadârand.* They don't like this sort of question. 6. *Nafahmidam cherâ javâb-i-ke dâdam dorost nist.* I didn't understand why the answer I gave wasn't right. 7. *Shomâ hamânjâ bemânid-o in chizhâ-râ barâyetân man miâvaram.* You stay right there, and I'll bring these things to you. 8. *Hamin emruz bekharid! Hafte-ye âyande qaymatesh kamtar nakhâhad bud.* Buy today! Next week the price of it won't be less.

(ج) ۱ همیشه خوشحال باشید. ۲ سؤال شما را درست نفهمیدند. ۳ این چیزها را برای آن پیرزنها بیرون ببرید. ۴ سه دفعه گم شدیم که به آن ده میرفتیم (وقتی که به آن ده میرفتیم سه دفعه گم شدیم). ۵ از این نوع قهوه را دوست ندارم. ۶ هفتهٔ گذشته با دوستانم صحبت میکردم. ۷ از ماجراهائی که در ایران داشتید برای من تعریف کنید. ۸ (یک) چند روز(ی) در شیراز گذراندیم. ۹ دیشب آبی که در آن ظرف بود یخ بست. ۱۰ این کاردها و چنگالها را ببرید و روی میز بگذارید.

Review III

(b) 1. *Ân qazâ-ye khoshmaze-i-râ-ke diruz be mâ dâdid khodetân dorost-karde-budid?* Did you yourself make that delicious food you gave us last night? 2. *Ân mard-e pir-i-ke haminjâ kâr-mikard, esmesh-râ farâmush-kardeam.* I have forgotten the name of that old man who used to work here. 3. *Dar hamin otâq kam-i bemânid-o darsetân-râ bekhânid.* Stay in this room for a while and study your lesson. 4. *Ân ketâb-e kohne-râ nemikhâham chonke midânam ke mofid nist.* I don't want that old book because I know it isn't useful. 5. *Chon hafte-ye âyande barâdaram az ân shahr-e dur-i-ke dar ânjâ kâr-mikonad miâyad, khâharam ham az jâ-i-ke dar ân englisi dars midehad barmigardad.* Since my brother is coming next week from the distant city in which he works, my sister is also returning from the place where she teaching English. 6. *Bâr-e avval-i-ke ânhâ-râ didam, nemidânam kay bud.* I don't know when the first time I saw them was. 7. *Te'dâd-e dâneshjuyân-i-ke dar in dâneshgâh dars mikhânand chist?* What is the number of students who study in this university? 8. *Ba'dan fahmidam ke cherâ mariz shodam: hatman az chiz-i bud ke khorde-budam.* Afterwards I understood why had got sick. It must have been from something I had eaten. 9. *Hichvaqt kârhâ-i-râ-ke barâ-ye man kardeid farâmush-nemikonam.* I will never forget the things you have done for me. 10. *Hichvaqt darbâre-ye qaymat-i-ke barâ-ye ân chizhâ dâdeast sohbat nakhâhad kard.* He will never talk about the price he paid for those things.

(ب) ۱ به حرفهای او گوش نکنید. ۲ برای اطاقی که در آن زندگی میکند زیاد میدهد. ۳ در خانه‌شان نه تا اطاق هست. ۴ پارسال ما اصلاً مریض نشدیم. ۵ آن کسانی که قبلاً دیدیم ایرانی نبودند؟ ۶ حرفهای مرا فراموش نکنید. ۷ نمیدانم چرا از آنها میترسید. ۸ هنوز نیامده بودم که برگشت و رفت. ۹ به خانه رفته بودند که شما رسیدید. ۱۰ در ربع ساعت چند دقیقه هست؟

Exercise 16

(الف) ۱ امکان دارد که من نیایم. ۲ شما باید این رنگ را تغییر بدهید. ۳ میخواهید اینها را گم کنید؟ ۴ همین حالا نمیتوانم فکر کنم. ۵ تو هیچوقت نباید در آنجا نگاه کنی. ۶ نتوانستند آن را بفروشند. ۷ نمیخواهید آن در را ببندید؟ ۸ من شاید او را دوست داشته باشم. ۹ میتوانند فارسی حرف بزنند. ۱۰ لازم نیست که او باز بیاید. ۱۱ من هم میخواهم کمی بردارم. ۱۲ میتواند خوب بشنود. ۱۳ میتوانی مرا ببینی؟ ۱۴ میخواستند اینها را دور بیندازند. ۱۵ شاید ما زورتر برسیم. ۱۶ بعداً خواستیم وارد شهر بشویم. ۱۷ نمیتوانم از آن ماجرا تعریف کنم. ۱۸ میخواهید آن قهوه را بخورید؟ ۱۹ نمیتوانم این در را باز کنم. ۲۰ نمیخواهد آن چیزها را به من بدهد. ۲۱ ما باید آنها را همراه بیاوریم. ۲۲ این شاید درست باشد. ۲۳ ممکن نیست من چنین غذائی را بخورم. ۲۴ میخوهند که ما بخانه برگردیم.

1. It's possible that I won't come. 2. You should change this color. 3. Do you want to lose these? 4. I can't think right now. 5. You should never look in there. 6. They couldn't sell it. 7. Don't you want to close that door? 8. I may love him/her. 9. They can speak Persian. 10. It is not necessary for him to come again. 11. I also want to take (pick up) a little bit. 12. He can hear well. 13. Can you see me? 14. They wanted to throw these things away. 15. We may arrive earlier. 16. Afterwards we were about to enter the city. 17. I cannot tell about that adventure. 18. Do you want to drink that coffee? 19. I cannot open this door. 20. He doesn't want to give me those things. 21. We have to bring them along. 22. This may be right. 23. It isn't possible for me to eat such food. 24. They

want us to return home.

(ب) ۱ نمیخواهم فردا به آنجا بروم. ۲ خواست آنرا دور بیندازد. ۳ میخواستیم چیزهائی‌را که دیروز گم کردیم پیدا کنیم. ۴ این کار چنان ساده است که نباید فکر کنم. ۵ فکر میکنم که از غذائی که در ده خوردم مریض شدم. ۶ نتوانستید جواب درستی به سؤال بدهید؟ ۷ میخواستم درست جواب بدهم، ولی نتوانستم. ۸ نگذار برادر کوچکت گم شود. ۹ چرا نمیگذارید من درِرا برای آنها باز کنم؟ ۱۰ نمیخواستید برای خودتان کفش و جوراب بخرید؟

Supplementary Vocabulary Practice

۱ دامن سبزی پوشیده است. ۲ امروز صبح پیژامه‌امرا درآورده‌ام. ۳ امروز پولور نپوشیده‌اید؟ ۴ امروز صبح زیرپیراهن نپوشیدم. ۵ بارانیتان‌را بپوشید. ۶ چرا با آن شلوار جوراب سبزی پوشیده‌اید؟ ۷ در آن وقت پالتو نپوشیده بودم. ۸ همیشه بلوز سفیدی میپوشد. ۹ میخواهم کفشهایم‌را درآوردم. ۱۰ صبحها لباسم‌را میپوشم و شبها درمیآورم.

Lesson 17

(الف) ۱ من از آن چیزها خوشم میآید. ۲ شما از این مطلب خوشتان نیامده است. ۳ ما از خوابیدن خوشمان میآید. ۴ محمد از کارتان خوشش نیامد. ۵ دانشجویان از زبان فارسی خوششان میآید. ۶ زهرا از درس خواندن خوشش نمی‌آمد. ۷ من از آن ساعت دیواری خوشم میآید. ۸ آنها از غذای ایرانی خوششان میآید. ۹ شما از چنان کارهائی خوشتان نمیآید. ۱۰ تو از آن شهر کوچک خوشت آمده بود.

(ب) ۱ دیشب ساعتِ یازده خوابیدم. ۲ دیشب هشت ساعت خوابیدم. ۳ معمولاً شبی هفت ساعت میخوابم. ۴ بله، امیدوار است به آنجا برگردد. نخیر، امیدوار نیست به آنجا برگردد. ۵ بله، رضا خوابش برده است. نخیر، رضا خوابش نبرده است. ۶ معمولا ساعت دوازده شب خوابم میآید. ۷ بله، میتوانند این مطالب‌را بفهمند. ۸ میخواهد روی تختخواب دراز بکشد. ۹ چرا، دوست دارم فارسی صحبت کنم. ۱۰ بله، احتمال دارد که آنها باز بیایند. نخیر، احتمال ندارد که آنها باز بیایند. ۱۱ بله، میخواهم اینهارا دور بیاندازم. نخیر، نمیخواهم اینهارا دور بیاندازم. ۱۲ دیشب به من خیلی خوش گذشت.

(c) 1. *Omidvâr budam emshab Layli-o Zahrâ-râ bebinam.* I was hopeful I would

18

Leili and Zahra tonight. 2. *Emkân dârad ke man emruz pish-e pezeshk beravam.* It is possible that I will go to the doctor today. 3. *Ma'mulan Javâd az qazâ-ye farangi khoshesh miâyad.* Javad usually likes European food. 4. *Lâzem nist ân chizhâ-râ be mâ neshân bedehand.* It is not necessary for them to show us those things. 5. *Bâyad hame-ye zarfhâ-râ be âshpazkhâne bebarim.* We have to take all the dishes into the kitchen. 6. *Ehtemâl dârad ke man emshab zud bekhâbam.* It is probable that I will go to bed early tonight. 7. *Emruz sobh be u goftam ke behtarin lebâshâ-yesh-râ bepushad.* I told him this morning to put on his best clothes. 8. *Az zud-residan bad-esh miâyad.* He dislikes arriving early. 9. *Momken-ast ke Rezâ digar sar-e kelâs nayâyad.* It is possible that Reza will not come to class any more. 10. *Az didan-e dustân-e irâni-am-o sohbat-kardan(-e) bâ ânhâ khosh-am miâyad.* I like to see my Iranian friends and talk with them.

(د) ۱ هفتهٔ گذشته چیزهائی که میخواستم بالاخره رسید. ۲ امکان دارد که ما وارد آن ساختمان بشویم؟ ۳ شک دارم که جواد بتواند جواب سؤالتانرا بدهد. ۴ رضا میخواست نیم ساعتی روی تختخواب دراز بکشد. ۵ اقلا دفعهٔ سوم است که این کاررا میکنیم. ۶ هنوز روزنامهرا برنداشته بودم که دیدم مال دیروز است. ۷ آن ایرانیای که دیشب (اورا) با شما دیدم کیست؟ ۸ امیدوارم که دیگر به اینجا نیایند. ۹ چرا میخواهید در آن خانهٔ قدیمی زندگی کنید؟ ۱۰ میخواهم لباسمرا درآورم و بخوابم.

Lesson 18

(الف) ۱ میتوان حدس زد. ۲ نباید فراموش کرد. ۳ نمیشود از اینها ترسید. ۴ باید از آن ماجرا تعریف کرد. ۵ ساعت یازده شب باید خوابید. ۶ نمیتوان امیدوار بود. ۷ نتوانست آن مطلبرا فهمید. ۸ نمیشود اینجا نشست. ۹ نباید حرفهای اورا باور کرد. ۱۰ باید همهٔ اینهارا پیش من برد.

(ب) ۱ آن اتفاق افتاده همه برگشتند. ۲ ما برا افتاده او و در خانه ماند. ۳ واقعهٔ مهمی پیش آمده نتوانستند بیایند. ۴ آنرا خودم دیده باور نمیکنم. ۵ لیلی هنوز نرسیده آنها دراه افتادند. ۶ وارد اطاق شده نشستند. ۷ به شهر برگشته همیشه آنجا میمانیم. ۸ اورا شناخته پیشش رفتیم.

(c) 1. *Vaqt-i-ke fahmidand ke shomâ nemikhâhid beravid, khodeshân be râh oftâdand.* When they realized that you didn't want to come, they set out themselves.

2. *Midânestam ke hatman vâqe'e-ye khayli mohemm-i pish-âmade-ast.* I knew that something very important must have happened. 3. *Didam ke shomâ dar ân sâkhtemân zendegi-mokonid.* I saw that you were living in that building. 4. *Hads-zad ke cherâ hanuz nayâmade-and.* He guessed why they hadn't come yet. 5. *Goftam ke nemishavad harfhâyesh-râ bâvar-kard.* I said it wasn't possible to believe what he said. 6. *Midânestam ke ân ettefâq-i-ke hamishe az ân mitarsidam khâhad oftâd.* I knew the thing I always feared would happen. 7. *Shenidam ke hamsâyegân momken-ast qabl az fardâ bargardand.* I heard it was possible the neighbors would come back before tomorrow. 8. *Az kojâ midânestid ke zemestân-e sard-i khâhad bud?* How did you know it would be a cold winter? 9. *Khayli ba'id-ast ke ân ettefâq-i-ke miguid bioftad.* It is very unlikely that the thing you are talking about will happen. 10. *Lebâs-am-râ darâvorde-o ru-ye takhtekhâb darâz-keshide khâbam bord.* I took off my clothes, stretched out on the bed, and fell asleep.

(د) ۱ میتوان حدس زد که همه خوابیده‌اند. ۲ حالا نمیتوان آن چیزها را به شما نشان داد. ۳ نمیتوان در آن ده کوچک گم شد. ۴ من از این رنگ خوشم نمیآید. ۵ آن چیزهای کهنه را دور بیندازیم؟ ۶ باور میکنید که چنان اتفاقی افتاد؟ ۷ کجا میخواهید بنشینید؟ ۸ شهلا گفت که امشب به خانهٔ شما میآید؟ ۹ به حسن گفتم که شما باور نمیکنید. ۱۰ ندانستیم که اتفاقی افتاده است (که واقعه‌ای پیش آمده است).

Exercise 19

(الف) ۱ علی و رضا باید دیروز رفته باشند. ۲ خیلی بعید است چنان واقعه‌ای پیش آمده باشد. ۳ فکر نمیکنم آن اتفاقی که میگفتید افتاده باشد. ۴ امکان دارد آنها قبل از ما براه افتاده باشند. ۵ امیدوارم که محمد آنها را به شما نشان داده باشد. ۶ نمیتوانید این چیزها را ارزان خریده باشید. ۷ همسایه‌هایتان باید جای دیگری رفته باشند. ۸ آن آقا باحتمال قوی باید دو روز پیش برگشته باشد. ۹ ممکن نیست که من وارد خانهٔ شما شده باشم. ۱۰ او شاید آنها را کشته باشد. ۱۱ شما نمیتوانید این را قبلاً دیده باشید. ۱۲ امکان ندارد که ما اینهمه را یاد گرفته باشیم. ۱۳ تنها چیزی که آنها ممکن است ندیده باشند این است. ۱۴ شما شاید یادتان رفته باشد. ۱۵ نمیتواند این کار را کرده باشد بجز اینکه خوب یاد گرفته باشد.

1. Ali and Reza must have gone yesterday. 2. It is very unlikely that such an event took place. 3. I don't think the event you were talking about happened. 4. It is possible that they got under way before us. 5. I hope that Mohammad has shown them to you. 6. You cannot have bought these things cheaply. 7. Your

neighbors must have gone somewhere else. 8. With great probability that gentleman should have returned two days ago. 9. It is not possible for me to have entered your house. 10. He may have killed them. 11. You cannot have seen this before. 12. It isn't possible for us to have learned all this. 13. This is the only thing it is possible they have not seen. 14. You may have forgotten. 15. He cannot have done this thing unless he has learned it well.

(b) 1. *Tanhâ vâqe'e-i-ke pish âmad ziâd mohemm nabud.* The only thing that happened was not very important. 2. *Ânqadr qaymathâ berân shode-ast ke magar in-ke âdam khayli puldâr bâshad nemitavânad kuchektarin chiz-i-râ bekharad.* Prices have become so expensive that unless one is very rich one cannot buy the smallest thing. 3. *Hads-zadam ke khayli ba'id-ast ânhâ-hâm hamchonân fekr-konand.* I guessed it was very unlikely they would think like that. 4. *Yâdetân naravad chand tâ tokhm-e morq az dokkân biâvarid.* Don't forget to bring a few eggs from the store. 5. *Mâshin-e mâ panj daqiqe râh narafte-bud ke deh-i-ke dar ân nâhâr khorde-budim nâpadid-shod.* Our car had not gone five minutes when the village in which we had eaten lunch disappeared from view. 6. *Fekr-mikardam ke hamânjâ neshaste-id.* I thought you were sitting over there. 7. *Be shart-i mitavânid beneshinid ke jâ bâshad.* You can sit down provided there is room. 8. *Pish az in-ke ân ja'behâ-râ bebandim, motma'enn bâshim ke hame chiz dorost-ast.* Before we close those boxes let's be sure that everything is right. 9. *Be u goftam ke hamânjâ beneshinad-o barnakhizad.* I told him to sit there and not get up. 10. *Sâ'at-e shesh-e ba'dazzohr-e bist-o-nohom-e esfandmâh-e hezâr-o-sisad-o-si-o-noh bud ke be Esfahân residim.* It was 6 P.M. on the 29th of Esfandmah 1339 when we arrived in Isfahan.

(ج) ۱ باید امروز صبح چیز بدی خورده باشم. ۲ نمیتواند مرده باشد، همین دیروز اورا دیدم. ۳ زندگانی او باید نسبةً آرام بوده باشد. ۴ نمیتوانید پارسال مرا دیده باشید مگر اینکه شما هم در ایران بوده باشید. ۵ برخیز (پاشو)! به شهر برویم. ۶ حتی بچه‌های اینجا پیر مینمایند، باید خیلی بد دیده باشند. ۷ علی نمیتواند خوابیده باشد. ۸ امکان ندارد که آنها همهٔ کتابهای مرا دور انداخته باشند. ۹ ساعت شش باید اینجا باشند مگر اینکه اتفاق بدی افتاده باشد. ۱۰ تنها چیزی که میدانم این است که در آن اطاق نشسته اند.

Exercise 20

(الف) ۱ دنبال کار جالبی میگردم که بکنم. ۲ ما سرگرم یاد گرفتنِ فارسی هستیم. ۳ فکر

میکنید که آنها بلندند جواب درستی بدهند؟ ۴ هرچند زندگانیت سخت باشد، باید امید
داشته باشی. ۵ بعد از رسیدنِ رضا، ما همه براه افتادیم. ۶ هر که چنین سؤالی‌را بکند، حتماً
خوب یاد نگرفته است. ۷ شما هر کجا آنهارا بگذارید، فرقی نمیکند. ۸ قبل از شناختنش
(قبل از آینکه بشناسمش) فکر میکردم کسی دیگر است. ۹ شما هرچه‌را که گم کرده باشید
باید پیدا کنید. ۱۰ سه ساعت پیش شروع کردم به خواندنِ این کتاب و هنوز هم میخوانم.
۱۱ چرا سعی میکنند جوانتر از آنکه هستند بنمایند؟ ۱۲ آنطور که او گریه میکند، باید
اتفاق خیلی بدی برایش افتاده باشد. ۱۳ آن بچه کوچکتر از آن است که از مدرسه برود.

1. I'm looking for something interesting to do. 2. We are busy learning Persian.
3. Do you think they know how to give a correct answer? 4. No matter how
difficult you life is, you should have hope. 5. After Reza arrived we all got under
way. 6. Anyone who asks such a question must not have learned well. 7. It
makes no difference where you put them. 8. Before recognizing him I thought
he was somebody else. 9. You have to find anything you have lost. 10. I started
reading this book three hours ago, and I'm still reading. 11. Why do they try to
look younger than they are? 12. The way he is crying, something bad must have
happened to him. 13. That child is too young to go to school.

(ب) ۱ هر که آنرا گفته باشد حتما بلد نیست. ۲ هر کاری بکنید و هر کجا بروید، دنبال شما
میگردند. ۳ سعی میکنم از دوستانم که در ایرانند برای شما تعریف کنم. ۴ زهرا زرنگتر از
آنست که به حرفهای او گوش کند. ۵ قبل از آمدنِ اینجا، اتفاقاً چیزی‌را که (شاید) به درد
شما بخورد پیدا کردم. ۶ از یاد گرفتنِ چیزهائی که قبلاً نمیدانستم خوشم میآید. ۷ سعی
میکند کاری‌را پیدا کند که امشب بکند. ۸ این به درد شما نمیخورد مگر اینکه خوب یاد
بگیرید. ۹ فکر نمیکنم فیلم شروع شده باشد و تآتر دور نیست. ۱۰ قبل از برخاستن شروع
کرد به صحبت کردن (شروع به صحبت کرد).

Review IV

(b) 1. *Hich khosham nemiâyad dombâl-e chonin chizhâ-i begardam.* I don't like to
look for such things. 2. *Nemitavânid hads bezanid mâ kojâ budeim.* You can't guess
where we have been. 3. *Har vaqt vâred-e khâne-ye u mishavand, maghqul-e kâr-e
digar-i-st.* Every time they enter his house he is busy with something else. 4. *Na
qam-khordanetân na gerye-kardanetân fâyede dârad.* Neither your grieving nor
your crying will do any good. 5. *Ma'mulan nemishavad inhâ-râ taqyir dâd.* It isn't
usually possible to change these. 6. *Nemitavânid ishân-râ qablan dide-bâshid.* You
can't have seen them before. 7. *Momken-ast ânhâ behtar az shomâ balad bâshand.*

It is possible that they know better than you. 8. *Bâvar-mikonid ke emkân dârad ke u-ham chonin kâr-i-râ karde-bâshad?* Do you believe it is possible for him to have done such a thing? 9. *Kâr-e mâ ziâd pish narafte-bud ke fahmidim pul-e bishtar-i lâzem-ast.* Our work had not progressed much when we realized we needed some more money. 10. *Sa'y-kon pish az bargashtan-e pedar-et in chizhâ-râ dur andâkhte-bâshi.* Try to have all these things thrown away before your father comes back.

(ج) ۱ نمیخواهید فردا زود براه بیافتید؟ ۲ هرکجا اینهارا پیدا کرده باشید، با من فرقی نمیکند. به من بدهید! ۳ قبل از اینکه برخیزید، اینرا بگویم. ۴ نمیتوانیم پیش برویم. حالا چه کار کنیم؟ ۵ یادتان رفته است که آن چیزهارا دور بیندازید؟ ۶ امکان دارد که آنجا به شما خوش بگذرد. ۷ گفت که میآید ولی فکر نمیکنم راهرا بلد باشد. ۸ معمولاً ساعتِ چند میخوابند؟ ۹ نمیخواهد از آن ماجرا تعریف کند. ۱۰ دیگر ترا دوست ندارم.

Exercise 21

(الف) ۱ اگر فردا باران ببارد (بارید)، ما نمیتوانیم برویم بیرون. ۲ اگر دیروز باران میبارید، ما نمیتوانستیم برویم بیرون. ۳ اگر دیروز میرفتید، من هم همراهتان میآمدم. ۴ اگر فردا بروید، من هم همراهتان میآیم. ۵ اگر خودت بلد بودی، چرا از من پرسیدی؟ ۶ اگر از من بپرسد، به او میگویم چکار بکند. ۷ اگر شما چراغهارا دوشن بکنید (کردید)، بهتر میبینیم. ۸ اگر فردا هوا خوب باشد (بود)، من اینهارا میشویم. ۹ اگر ما خانهٔ بزرگتری داشتیم، بهتر بود. ۱۰ اگر همینجا روی تختخواب دراز بکشم، حالم بهتر میشود. ۱۱ اگر تو خاموش نشوی، من ترا میکشم.

1. If it rains tomorrow, we won't be able to go out. 2. If it had been raining yesterday, we wouldn't have been able to go out. 3. If you had gone yesterday, I would have come with you. 4. If you go tomorrow, I'll come with you. 5. If you knew how, why did you ask me? 6. If he asks me, I'll tell him what to do. 7. If you turn on the lights, we'll see better. 8. If the weather is good tomorrow, I'll wash these. 9. If we had a larger house, it would be better. 10. If I stretch out for a little while on the bed, I'll feel better. 11. If you don't shut up, I'll kill you!

(ب) ۱ مریم و شیرین باید خیلی زودتر میرسیدند. ۲ بهتر بود مشغول کار خودتان میشدید. ۳ ما باید آنهارا ارزانتر میخریدیم. ۴ محمد باید قبلاً برمیگشت. ۵ شما بایستی آنهارا میدیدید. ۶ رضا میبایست بیشتر درس میخواند. ۷ آقا، میبایستی خیلی بیشتر از این کار میکردید. ۸ تو نمیبایست آن چراغرا خاموش میکردی. ۹ این نباید با شما فرق میکرد.

۱۰ بهتر بود من زودتر شروع میکردم.

1. Maryam and Shirin should have arrived much earlier. 2. It would have been better had you minded your own business. 3. We should have bought them more cheaply. 4. Mohammad should have returned before. 5. You should have seen them. 6. Reza should have studied more. 7. Sir, you should have worked much more than this. 8. You should have put that light out. 9. This should not have made a difference to you. 10. It would have been better for me to have started earlier.

(ب) ۱ خیلی وقت است حالش اینطور است. ۲ شش ماه است فارسی میخوانم. ۳ ده دقیقه است این چراغ روشن شده است. ۴ دو روز بود باران میامد. ۵ (یک) چند هفته است دنبال چنین کاری میگردم. ۶ شش ماه است روغن ماشینم عوض نشده است. ۷ پنج هفته است برادران و خواهرانم را ندیده‌ام. ۸ خیلی وقت است میخواهند فارسی یاد بگیرند. ۹ پانزده سال است مدرسه میروم. ۱۰ دوازده ماه است در این شهر هستیم.

Exercise 22

(الف) ۱ درس خواندن > درس‌خوان studious.

۲ بردن > برنده winner.

۳ بار بردن > باربر porter.

۴ غم خوردن > غمخور griever.

۵ شستن > شوینده washer.

۶ لباس شستن > لباسشو clothes washer.

۷ کشتن > کشنده killer, killing.

۸ نمودن > نماینده representative.

۹ یاد گرفتن > یادگیر learner.

۱۰ بطری باز کردن > بطری‌بازکن bottle opener.

۱۱ کتاب فروختن > کتابفروش bookseller.

۱۲ عینک ساختن > عینکساز eyeglass-maker, optician.

۱۳ آدم کشتن > آدمکش murderer/murderous.

۱۴ دندان ساختن > دندان‌ساز (old-fashioned dentist) toothmaker.

24

(ج) ۱ از اطاق به اطاق روان چراغ دوشن میکرد. ۲ پرسان و پرسان بالاخره رسیدیم. ۳ روی تختخواب افتان شروع به گریه کرد. ۴ برخیزان شروع کردند به صحبت کردن. ۵ دراز کشان خوابم برد. ۶ بچه‌ها گریه کنان پیش مادرشان آمدند. ۷ همانطور حرف زنان برخاست و رفت.

(c) 1. *Fardâ sobh âmâde-ye raftan-e Tehrân bâshid!* Be ready to go to Tehran tomorrow morning. 2. *Hanuz nâhâremân-râ nakhorde-budim ke sedâ-ye mâshin-e Mohammad-râ shenidim ke miâmad.* We had not yet eaten lunch when we heard the sound of Mohammad's car coming. 3. *Agar piâde nemiâmadand-o bâ mâshin miâmadand, dir-nemikardand.* If they hadn't come on foot and had come by car, they wouldn't have been late. 4. *Behtar-ast bâ havâpaymâ beravim, yâ meshavad bâ mâshin-ham raft?* Would it be better for us to go by plane, or is it possible to go there by car? 5. *Qabl az inke bârân biâyad mâshin-râ nazdik-e deh-e kuchek-i negahdâshte-budim.* Before the rain came, we had stopped the car near a small village. 6. *Tawr-i-ke kâr-e mâ pish-miravad, tâ tamâm shavad mâ hame pir-shodeim.* The way our work is progressing, we'll all be old by the time it's finished. 7. *Zud bâsh! Nemikhâham dir-konam.* Be quick! I don't want to be late. 8. *Az bas-ke dir-kardeim, tâ be forudgâh veresim havâpaymâ rafte-ast.* We're so late, by the time we get to the airport the plane will have left. 9. *Yek-i az mashhurtarin âvâzkhânhâ-ye Irân Shajariân-ast.* One of the most famous singers in Iran is Shajarian. 10. *Sa'y-kardam cherâgh-râ rawshan-konam vali natavânestam kelid-esh-râ paydâ-konam.* I tried to put the light on, but I couldn't find the switch.

(د) ۱ ماشین را همینجا نگهدارید. میخواهم پیاده شوم. ۲ قبل از اینکه شام بخورید، یادتان نرود دستهایتان را بشوئید. ۳ حدس زدم که آن چیزها را دور نمی‌اندازند. ۴ قبل از ناهار خوردن خوشم میآید دراز بکشم و چند دقیقه بخوابم. ۵ گوینده چیزی میگوید. گوش کنیم. ۶ معمولاً قبل از اینکه چیزی از روی میزم بردارم می‌پرسم. ۷ تا به اینجا برسند همه چیز تمام شده است. ۸ نمیتوانیم شام بخوریم تا برادر و خواهرتان برسند (تا برادر و خواهرتان نرسند نمیتوانیم شام بخوریم). ۹ اگر پیاده بروید تا ساعت شش نمیرسید. ۱۰ شک دارم که قبل از اینکه هواپیما پرواز کند بتوانید به فرودگاه برسید.

Exercise 23

(a) 1. آقائی *âqâi* gentlemanliness. 2. بزرگی *bozorgi* largeness, greatness. 3. کوتاهی *kutâhi* shortness. 4. کوتاهقدی *kutâhqaddi* shortness of stature. 5. سادگی *sâdegi* simplicity. 6. زودی *zudi* quickness, earliness. 7. جوانی *javâni* youth. 8. خوشحالی *khoshhâli* happiness. 9. باربری *bârbari* transport (truck, e.g.), the job of being a porter 10. دانائی *dânâi* wisdom. 11. فراموشکاری *farâmushkâri* forgetfulness. 12. سختی *sakhti* difficulty. 13. دوری *duri* distance. 14. نزدیکی *nazdiki* nearness, proximity. 15. بدبختی *badbakhti* misfortune. 16. زودگذری *zudgozari* ephemerality. 17. پولداری *puldâri* wealth. 18. سفیدی *sefidi* whiteness. 19. کهنگی *kohnegi* oldness. 20. بخشندگی *bakhshandegi* generosity. 21. پیادهروی *piâderavi* walking, pedestrianism. 22. خوانائی *khânâi* readability, legibility. 23. برادرانگی *barâdarânegi* brotherliness. 24. معلمی *mu'allemi* the teaching profession. 25. مردمشناسی *mardomshenâsi* anthropology. 26. همسایگی *hamsâyegi* the state of being a neighbor, close proximity. 27. بچگانگی *bachchegânegi* childishness. 28. آسانی *âsâni* ease. 29. دوستی *dusti* friendship. 30. روزنامهنویسی *ruznâmenevisi* journalism

(b) 1. درسخوانی *darskhâni* studiousness. 2. برندگی *barandegi* being a winner. 3. باربری *bârbari* being a porter, transportation. 4. غمخوری *qamkhori* grieving, grief. 5. شویندگی *shuyandegi* being a washer, pertaining to washing. 6. لباسشوئی *lebâsshu'i* (the act of) clothes-washing, pertaining to washing clothes. 7. کشندگی *koshandegi* being a killer, lethality. 8. نمایندگی *nemâyandegi* representation. 9. یادگیری *yâdgiri* learning, the process of learning, pertaining to learning. 11. کتابفروشی *ketâbforushi* being a bookseller, a book shop. 12. عینکسازی *aynaksâzi* eyeglass-making. 13. آدمکشی *âdamkoshi* murder, murderousness, homicide. 14. دندانسازی *dandânsâzi* tooth-making, dentistry. 15. کمخوابی *kamkhâbi* sleeping little.

(ج) ١ چرا، آن نامههارا فرستادم. ٢ چرا، میآیند. ٣ نخیر، ندیدهام. ۴ چرا، میدانم این چیست. ۵ نخیر، آنقدر پول ندارم. ۶ بله، فارسی بلدم. ٧ چرا، آمادهام. ٨ بله، با ماشین میرویم. ٩ نخیر، ناهار نخوردم. ١٠ چرا، میدانم.

(d) 1. *Yek-i do tâ eshkâl dâshtim-o agarna zudtar miresidim.* We had a couple of problems; otherwise, we would have arrived earlier. 2. *Dar Irân har vaqt âdam-i moaddab vâred-e otâq mishavad bâyad be hame salâm-konad.* In Iran, every time a polite person enters a room, he has to greet everyone. 3. *Ânche ân devâne miguyad dard-e sar miâvarad.* What that crazy guy says gives (you, us, everybody) a headache. 4. *Del-am-ra shekastid vali bâz-ham qam-nemikhoram.* You broke my

26

heart, but I'm still not going to grieve. 5. *Be dars-khândanetan hatman edâme-dehid.* By all means continue your studying. 6. *Barâ-ye in kâr az che mikhâhid estefâde-konid?* What do you want to use for this job? 7. *Khânom, bebakhshid, vaqt-ast ke mâ bâ hamdigar khodâhâfezi-konim.* Madam, excuse me, but it's time for us to say good-bye to each other. 8. *Kas-i-ke chonin harfhâ-i-râ bâvar-konad bâyad khayli zudbâvar bâshad.* Anyone who believes such words must be very gullible. 9. *Man mikhâstam pezeshki bekhânam vali pedaram pishnehâd-kard ke dandânpezeshki bekhânam.* I wanted to study medicine, but my father suggested I study dentistry. 10. *Shab-i be ân siâhi hichvaqt nadide-budam. Khoshbakhtâne cherâq hamrâh-dâshtim.* Never had I seen a night so dark. Luckily we had a flashlight along.

(هـ) ١ سعی کنید این اطاقرا تمیز نگهدارید. ٢ این بیشتر بچگانگی است تا دیوانگی. ٣ مگر سعی نکردند ماشینرا نگهدارند؟ ۴ میتوان به آن شهرهای دور با هواپیما رسید؟ ۵ بعید است چنان اتفاقی دوباره بیفتد. ۶ میدانستیم که دیر میکنند. ٧ در این نزدیکیها جائی هست که امشب بخوابیم؟ ٨ مگر میخواهید به کسی که چنان کاریرا کرده باشد ببخشید؟ ٩ مگر به آقایان و خانمهائی که دیر آمدند سلام نکردید؟ ١٠ بهتر است که شما به کارتان ادامه بدهید، وگرنه هیچوقت تمام نمیکنید.

Exercise 24

(a) 1. *Be qadr-i khaste-am ke faqat mikhâham esterâhat-konam.* I am so tired I only want to rest. 2. *Bâzâr be qadr-i sholuq bud ke jâ-ye khâli paydâ-nemishod.* The market was so crowded that no empty space could be found. 3. *Harche teshnetar bâshi, âb khoshmazetar-ast.* The thirstier you are, the more delicious water is. 4. *Behtar-ast bâ mâshin veravim; agarna, man nemiâyam.* It would be better for us to go by car; otherwise, I'm not coming. 5. *Nazdik bud az gorosnegi-o teshnegi bemirim.* We nearly died of hunger and thirst. 6. *Vaqt-i-ke didam khâne-ye hamsâye âtesh gerefte-ast, be âteshneshâni telefon-kardam.* When I saw that the neighbor's house was on fire, I telephoned to the fire department. 7. *Hanuz dah kilometr-i az shahr narafte-budim ke mâshin-i ruberu-ye mâ istâd-o mard-i piâde shod.* Scarcely had we gone ten kilometers from the city when a car stopped opposite us and a man got out. 8. *Shomâ be nazar khaste miâid. Cherâ kam-i esterâhat-nemi-konid?* You look tired. Why don't you rest a bit?

(ب) ١ به او گفتیم که فردا صبح هرچه زودتر براه بیفتیم، بهتر. ٢ هرچه بیشتر سعی کردم آتشرا بنشانم، ولی فایده نداشت. ٣ هرچه زودتر آن نامهایرا که نوشتهاید بفرستید، زودتر

میرسد. ۴ قبل از اینکه باران بیاید در باغ گردشی بکنیم. ۵ باید اشکالی داشته باشند، وگرنه تا حالا میرسیدند. ۶ هیچوقت اطاقی به این کثیفی‌را ندیده‌ام! مگر فکر میکنید که من آن‌را تمیز میکنم؟ ۷ باید دیوانه باشد اگر فکر میکند که من دوباره این کار‌را میکنم. ۸ وارد شده خیلی مؤدبانه به همه چای تقدیم کرد. ۹ وقتی که رسیدم شیراز به نظر شلوغ آمد ولی به شلوغی تهران نیست. ۱۰ کمی از آن مایع ظرفشوئی در آب بریزید تا ظرفها تمیز درآید.

Reading passage:

Ân mard âmad-o pesarbachchehâ-i-râ ke khâna nadâshtand da'vat kard tâ bâ u be jâ-ye behtar-i beravand. Chon bachchehâ az u mahabbat dide-budand, bâ u raftand. Ân mard-e khub bachchehâ-râ be khâne-ye khodesh bord. Dar khâne-ye ân mard do mard-e khub-e digar-ham budand. Ânhâ be bachchehâ pul dâdand, shâm dâdand, rakhtekhâb-e garm-ham dâdand-o fardâ sobh be ânhâ goftand, "Agar mikhâhid hamishe dârâ-ye chonin zendegi bâshid, bâyad moti'-o farmânbardâr bâshid." Bachchehâ chon mahabbat dide-budand, qabul-kardand-o yek hafte-ye ba'd harkodâm dar yek noqte-ye shahr mashqule jibbori shodand-o ânche az ostâd âmukhte-budand dar mawqe'-e kâr be kâr mibordand-o âkher-e shabhâ bâ jib-e por be khâne barmigashtand-o harche kâr karde-budand be ân se mard-e khub taqdim-mikardand-o ruzgâreshân be khubi-o khoshi migozasht.

Yek ruz yek-i-shân gir-oftâd-o dar kalântari baqiye-râ-ham law-dâd. Ânhâ-râ mohâkeme-kardand-o be dârotta'dib ferestâdand. Se mâh dar dârotta'dib budand-o dar in moddat az digarân khayli chizhâ yâd-gereftand.

That man came and invited the boys, who had no homes, to go with him to a better place. Since the boys had seen affection from him, they went with him. That good man took the boys to his own house. In that man's house there were two other good men. They gave the boys money, dinner, and warm bedding, and the next morning they said to them, "If you want always to have such a life, you must be obedient and mindful." Since the boys had been treated affectionately, they accepted, and one week later each of them got busy pick-pocketing in a spot in the city, and while working they put into practice what they had learned from the master, and at the end of the evening they would return home with full pockets and present to those three good men what they had made, and their days passed pleasantly.

One day one of them got caught and informed on the others at the police station. They were sentenced and sent to the reformatory. They were in the reformatory for three months, and during that time they learned many things from the others.

Exercise 25

(الف) ۱ کتابم گم شد. ۲ اینها شسته نمی‌شود. ۳ ایشان روی زمین نشانده شده‌اند. ۴ آنچه کرده بود بخشیده نشد. ۵ این بکار برده نمی‌شود. ۶ آن خانه تازه ساخته شد. ۷ دلم شکسته شد. ۸ من مجبور شدم که همراهشان بروم. ۹ ماشین نگهداشته شده بود. ۱۰ آنها در این شهر پیدا نمی‌شود.

Reading Passage:

Moslem dar birun-e shahr-e Marv dar rustâ-ye Mâkhân zamin-i kharid-o khâne-i sâkht-o khânedân-e khod-râ dar ânjâ neshând. Dar sâl-e sad-o noh-e hejri ke Abdorrahmân be jahân âmad, rustâ-ye Mâkhân dar se-farsangi-e shahr-e Marv, ke in kudak dar ânjâ cheshm bâz karde-bud, bâ chand rustâ-ye digar az ân-e pedar-ash bud. Moslem, pedar-e Abdorrahmân, dar miân-e javânmardân-e Marv be maqâm-e besyâr boland-i reside-bud-o ishân be taw'-o raqbat u-râ be râhnemâi-o pishvâi-e khod ekhtiâr-karde-budand. Abdorrahmân dar in mohit-i javanmardi-o bozorgvâri, dar miân-e delâvarân-e ma'ruf-e Marv, roshd-karde-o kam-kam javân-e borumand-i shode-bud. Mardom-e Marv-o javânmardân-e ân diâr, pas az Moslem, omid-eshân be pesar-e rashid-e u bud ke, chon vâred-e zendegi shod, konye-ye Abu-Moslem-râ ekhtiâr-kard-o inak digar "Abu-Moslem Abdorrahmân-e Khorâsâni" dar hame-ye Khorâsân be javânmardi-o fotovvat-o bakhshandegi-o Irânparasti ma'ruf shod.

Dar in zamân javânmardân-e Marv pesarân-e khod-râ az khordsâli-o az hamân avval ke be dabirestân miraftand-o khatt miâmukhtand be maslak-o marâm-e khod âshnâ-mikardand-o az hamân âqâz-e zendegi, be âin-e Irân-e qadim, savâri-o tir-andâzi-o moshtzani-o shamshirzani-o kamandandâzi-o nayzeandâzi-o zubinbâzi-râ yâd-midâdand. Abdorrahmân-e javân dar in fonun az hamsâlân-e khod bartari-yâfte-bud.

Moslem bought some land outside the city of Marv in the village of Makhan, built a house, and settled his family there. In the year 109 of the Hegira, when Abdorrahman was born, the village of Makhan, three leagues from the city of Marv, in which he opened his eyes [to the world], along with several other villages, belonged to his father. Moslem, Abdorrahman's father, had attained a very high position among the nobles of Marv, and they willingly chose him as their leader. Abdorrahman grew up among renowned warriors of Marv in this environment of nobility and greatness, and little by little he became a worthy youth. After Moslem, the hopes of the people of Marv and the nobles of that region were in his eldest son, who, when he entered life, chose the name Abu-Moslem, and so "Abu-Moslem Abdorrahman of Khurasan" became known in all of Khurasan for nobility, chivalry, generosity, and patriotism.

At this time the nobles of Marv acquainted their sons with their careers and goals from the very beginning when they went to school and learned to write, and from that very beginning of life, in accordance with the custom of ancient Iran, they learned horsemanship, archery, boxing, sword-play, lasso-throwing, spear-throwing, and javelin play. The young Abdurrahman was superior to his contemporaries in these skills.

Reading Selections (Modern)

1

They say that in olden times a petty merchant from Kashan sold everything he had, took his wife by the hand, left Kashan, and kept going until he got to Tabriz. There he opened a kabob shop.

On the first day the shop was washed and swept out, the merchant from Kashan sat in expectation of customers, and after a few minutes four Tabrizi ruffians came into the shop and and ordered elaborate kabobs and ate them with bread. As they were leaving the shop they said to the owner of the shop in an imperious manner, "Hey! Let's not have any talk about money. Don't make a peep! If you want to be safe, you'll have to take care of us every day like this. And for free. Understand? Otherwise we'll 'get' you!"

This they said and departed. The poor Kashi in fear immediately closed the shop, left Tabriz with his wife, and kept going until he got to his own town and region, i.e. Kashan. As soon as he entered his former house he said to his wife, "Shut the door tight!" She shut it. The man from Kashan went up on the roof, stood facing the city of Tabriz, and, waving his hands up and down, shouting and in anger, cursed the ruffians of Tabriz. And he added vindictively, "I'll get you! You think you can scare me!!"

From inside the courtyard his wife cried out, "Dear, come down! Do you want to start a blood feud?"

2

I had bought half a kilo of mutton and was proceeding carefully down one side of the street when a friend came up to me, and after some chit-chat and asking how each other was, I saw he had prescription glasses, or as they say, magnifying glasses, on his eyes.

I said with astonishment, "So-and-so, there isn't anything wrong with your eyes, is there?"

"No," he said, "but one of my eyes had become somewhat weak and didn't see things correctly, and I couldn't read the newspaper right. There wasn't anything

30

to be done but to consult the eye-doctor, and it turned out that my left eye was weak, so the doctor gave me these glasses to put on my eyes." He said good-bye and left.

After my friend's departure I felt one of my eyes was weak. What did it mean? Until a few moments ago it had been fine. How could it have grown weak in just a few seconds? I thought for a bit to figure out which of my eyes was weak. I couldn't figure out anything. There was nothing to be done, so I stopped right there on the edge of the sidewalk and put the package of meat down on the ground. I closed my left eye and took aim at a crow that was sitting on a radio antenna on the roof of the house opposite. I saw that it was OK. I could see the crow perfectly. Its color was black, its beak was as it should be, and I could see its feet well. I was relieved that my right eye wasn't faulty, and whatever defect there was was in my left eye.

I put my palm over my right eye and took aim at the crow with my left eye. Involuntarily my heart sank. My head began to hurt, and my temples started throbbing. The crow's neck had become short, I couldn't see its beak right, its feet were blurred, and its color was gray. What did it mean? I became nervous. At once I took my hand from my right eye and covered my left eye. I saw I could see all right. The crow was the same crow as before, but it wasn't possible to give up on this medical experiment so soon, was it?

I put the package of meat on the ground, leaned against the wall on the avenue sidewalk, and now, without getting help from my palms, I began to experiment by closing and opening my eyelids. As bad luck would have it, the crow that was the object of my aim and experiment, took fright at something—I don't know what—and flew away, and I was left without a target. I began to look around to find a new target, but I had become so flustered that my right eye no longer worked. Finally I found a sparrow that was sitting on an electric wire on the avenue at a distance of three hundred meters and immediately experimented with my right eye. I saw that there was no question of its being a sparrow, but it was somewhat smaller, and when I looked with my left eye all I could see on the wire was a black speck. I bore absolutely no resemblance whatsoever to a sparrow. I called out to a man who was passing by me and said, "Brother, if it's no trouble, close one of your eyes."

The guy, who had no idea what was going on, gave me a meaningful look and, before acting on my order and closing one of his eyes, grabbed his pocket flaps tightly and then asked, "Why?"

"What's it to you?" I said. "Close it."

The fellow, who thought I wanted either to pick his pockets or to show him one of Professor Shandou's or Mirza Malkom Khan's tricks, stood in front of me and shut one of his eyes. "Now turn your back to me," I said, "and see what you see on the wire on the other side of the avenue." He gave me another of those meaningful looks, turned his head in the direction I had indicated, and said, "Nothing."

I saw this poor guy was blinder than I was. I asked, "Isn't there anything on the wire?"

"No," he said.

"You blind fool," I said, "I can see it with my one good eye. How come you don't see it?"

"It's your father who's blind! It's your mother who's blind!" he said. "OK, I don't see anything. Do I have to?"

I shut one of my eyes and looked at the wire with my other eye. I saw that I too didn't see anything. I shut my defective eye and looked with my sound eye. Still I didn't see anything. I got upset, thinking that, God forbid, both of my eyes had become defective."

The guy said angrily, "OK, what's your point? What thing do you want me to see?"

"There was a sparrow on that wire," I said. "Now I don't see it."

He drew himself back and said, "It must have flown away. Was the sparrow yours?"

"No," I said. "Where would I get a sparrow from?" He crooked his index finger, tapped his temples several times, and said, "If you had a sound mind, you'd be better off." And he went on his way.

3

One hot summer day, one thirteenth of Mordad to be precise, at around 2:45 PM, I fell in love. Many times the bitterness and pangs of separation I experienced made me think that if it had been a twelfth or a fourteenth of Mordad, it might not have turned out the way it did.

That day, like every day, they had sent us, meaning me and my sister, with pressure, force, threats, and some promises for nice things in the late afternoon, into the basement to sleep. In the severe heat of Tehran afternoon naps were obligatory for all children. But that day too, like every other afternoon, we were waiting for father to fall asleep so we could go out into the garden to play. When the sound of father's snoring grew loud, I brought my head out from under the sheet and looked at the wall clock. It was 2:30 PM. My poor kid sister had fallen asleep while waiting for father to go to sleep. There wasn't anything I could do but tiptoe out by myself.

My uncle's daughter Leyli and her little brother had been waiting for us in the garden for half a hour. There was no wall between our houses, which had been built in a large garden. Like every day we busied ourselves talking and playing under a large walnut tree without making any noise. All of a sudden my gaze fell upon Leyli's. A pair of huge black eyes were looking at me. I couldn't detach my gaze from Leyli's. I don't know how long we had been staring at one another when suddenly my mother loomed over our heads with a switch made from several branches. Leyli and her brother ran off to their house, and my mother, threatening me, took me back to the basement and under the sheet. Before my head disappeared completely beneath the sheet my eye fell upon the wall clock. It was 2:50 PM. Before putting her own head under the sheet in her turn, my mother said, "Thank God your uncle didn't wake up. Otherwise he would've chopped you all to pieces!"

My mother was right. Uncle was very fanatical about the orders he gave. He had ordered that children should not even breathe before five o'clock in the afternoon. Within the four walls of the garden not only had we children had a taste of what it meant not to sleep in the afternoon and to make a racket while Uncle was asleep but the crows and pigeons too showed up less during that period because Uncle had exterminated them several times with a shotgun. Itinerant peddlers did not pass through the lane that bore Uncle's name until around five o'clock because the muleteer who sold melons and the onion seller had gotten slapped several times by Uncle.

However, that day my mind was very occupied, and the mention of Uncle's name did not bring to mind memories of his fights and bad moods. Not for a moment could I get free of the memory of Leyli's eyes and her gaze, and no matter how I tossed and turned, no matter what I tried to think of, I saw her black eyes even brighter than if she had really been in front of me.

Again at night within the mosquito net Leyli's eyes came in search of me. I hadn't seen her again that afternoon, but her eyes and caressing gaze were there. I don't know how much time passed. Suddenly a strange thought took hold of my whole mind: O God! Don't let me have fallen in love with Leyli! I tried to laugh at this thought of mine, but no laughter came. It is possible for one not to laugh at a stupid thought, but that doesn't mean it isn't stupid. It isn't possible to fall in love without any preliminaries, is it?

I tried to review the entirety of my information about love. Regrettably that information was not vast. Although more than thirteen years of my life had passed, until that moment I had not seen a single person in love. Few romantic books or biographies of lovers had been published at that time. Moreover, they wouldn't allow us to read any of them. Mother, father, and the relatives, especially Uncle, the shadow of whose existence and whose ideas and beliefs loomed over the heads of all members of the family, forbade us children to go out without a chaperone, and we didn't dare go near the street kids. The radio too, which had not been in operation long, had no important matter in its two or three hours of daily programming that would help to enlighten the mind.

In the review of my information about love I came across in the first instance Leyli and Majnoun, whose story I had heard many times. However, no matter how hard I scraped the corners of my mind, I saw that I hadn't heard anything about the manner in which Majnoun had fallen in love with Leyli. They just said Majnoun fell in love with Leyli.

It probably would have been better altogether in this inventory had I not gotten Leyli and Majnoun involved because the fact that Leyli and my cousin had the same name probably, without my knowing it myself, was influential in my later conclusions. However, I had no choice. The most important lovers known to me were Leyli and Majnoun. Other than them, I didn't know much about Shirin and Farhad, especially about the manner in which they fell in love. I had read a romantic story that had been printed at the bottom of a newspaper, but I had not read the first couple of installments and one of my classmates had told me about it. Consequently I didn't know the beginning of the adventure.

I heard the sound of the basement wall clock striking twelve. O God! It was midnight, and I had not yet gone to sleep. For as long as I could remember that clock had been in our house, but this was the first time I heard it strike twelve midnight. Maybe this sleeplessness was also an indication of my having fallen in love. In the semi-darkness of the courtyard, where, from behind the mosquito net, I saw the shadows of the trees and rose bushes as strange, fantastic phantoms, I was terrified because, before I could come to a conclusion about having fallen in love or not, I was scared by the fates of the lovers I had reviewed. Almost all of them had tragic fates, and the adventure had ended in death and dying.

Leyli and Majnoun—death and dying. Shirin and Farhad—death and dying. Romeo and Juliet—death and dying. Paul and Virginie—death and dying. That story in the newspaper—death and dying.

O God! Don't let me really have fallen in love, and don't let me die too!

4

One morning when I awoke from sleep I saw the situation of my room and house different from every other day. The city in which I used to live was in a region where date trees could be kept only in pots, and in the winter it was absolutely necessary to move them along with the other flower pots into covered greenhouses and protected rooms. However, that morning, when, as usual, I tossed and turned this way and that a bit, yawned, and looked around before getting out of bed, I looked out of the window, my eye fell upon tall date palms, the branches of which were moving in the strong wind inside the courtyard, and farther away the tops of many date trees could be seen. No, I wasn't having a dream. I wasn't watching a film. It was I myself who had woken up from sleep and was seeing with my own two eyes in the world of wakefulness date trees outside whose branches were trembling in the wind and the sound of the rustling of which was reaching my ears.

My house was a large enclosure that mostly resembled an abandoned and forgotten garden, in the middle of which was situated a wide building with a row of short, square columns such that the floors of the rooms were level with the ground of the courtyard. The ground that was all around the building had, some years previously, been divided into plots, but the only trees worth mentioning were those date trees whose thick, knotted trunks with their brown fibers could be seen here and there like columns. In a corner of the garden, near a hole that was situated at the bottom of the wall and may have been an entrance or exit for water, several crooked trees, the branches of which were bent to the ground, displayed themselves. In the garden plots many wild weeds had sprung up and it was like a desert whose springtime grasses had dried up from the heat of the burning summer sun.

5

When he fell into the bed and, as usual, picked up the newspaper and pencil, he saw that he couldn't solve the puzzle. There was a ringing in his ears, and the puzzle, with its black and white squares, both of which were dazzling and glittered with an annoying light, hurt his eyes. His gaze was upon the newspaper, but he could see the faces of the Tehranis and Mortaza Khan and hear their laughter and derisive words. He knew how meaningless, silly, and stupid this thing he did was in their view, and he knew further that, other than this, he wasn't capable of doing anything. As though being obstinate to them or to himself, he determined to solve the puzzle down to the last square. Of all the things in the world he was capable of doing only this, and he wanted to prove to himself that at least he could do it.

With obstinacy he read the clues and applied pressure to his brain. He wanted to guess the right word and not mess up the puzzle with his mistakes. But the various words, like embers jumping from glowing coals, flew from the corners and edges of his mind and went out before he could grab them or see them. He head was spinning. The ringing in his ears had become annoying. His eyelids were getting heavy and coming together. As he strove to keep them open, an unendurable pain was pulling his eyeballs out. His whole body had become weak, and he almost collapsed altogether. His hands, which held the newspaper and the pencil, were tingling. He wanted to let go of the newspaper and pencil and throw himself, limp and listless, onto the ground.

He had become dizzy, weak, and impatient. It was as though he had been bound with a chain and was being pulled from all sides. All at once he began to weep with helplessness. He sobbed. He was bent over on himself, his shoulders were trembling, and tear drops were streaming from under his glasses, dripping and spreading on the squares of the puzzle and making the ink dark.

He felt that he was of no use for anything in this world, useless, futile. He didn't know how to do anything, and even the few trivial things he did know he couldn't accomplish or make use of to make his life a little more comfortable or pleasant. He wished there were someone on whose shoulders he could put his head and weep as much as he could, and that person would comfort him and console him. But he had no one.

Even his wife, who was sleeping with her mouth open on the other side and breathing noisily, was so sound asleep that she did not wake up with the sound of his crying. He was alone. He was sitting alone, weeping in helplessness. In the end the newspaper and pencil fell from his hands, and his eyelids came together from exhaustion and heaviness. Before he fell completely asleep he was only able to take his glasses off.

6

After performing the noon prayer in the large mosque in the market, the man came out, took a road, and went to one of the quarters of the city. The children grew happy at seeing an unfamiliar, strange being, everything about whom possessed novelty for them, and fell in after him. A few clowns and acrobats, whose market was experienced a slump, thinking they would be able to make use of his existence to drum up trade for themselves, joined them. Some curious people, out of curiosity naturally, and beggars—perhaps because of a feeling they had of having a fate in common with this poor newcomer, who looked a little crazy—joined in with the crowd. The young man did not know what to do with them. He said to himself, "It's certain that I won't get past them in one piece, and no matter what I say, they will grow bolder." Thus it was that he decided to be bold and stand his ground and have nothing to do with them. Of every person he encountered he asked the whereabouts of Shaykh Baha'i and his house and said he had urgent business with him.

In a few places one or two people thought they could fool him. They called themselves or someone else Shaykh Baha'i, but the laughter and uproar of the crowd of idle people and onlookers spoiled the joke, and the young man kept on knocking obstinately and calmly at the door of every house, stopping every person and repeating his question.

At one point he came to a cramped, narrow lane where several poor, skinny villagers were displaying for sale the fruits they had placed on donkeys skinnier than themselves. The road had came to an end. Everyone stopped. The young man approached an old man who was buying fruit. He asked him to answer his question. The children and idlers stared out from behind him. A few people poked their heads out. The doors of one or two houses opened and closed. Then the crowd dispersed like snow melting. The children, for whom the affair no longer held any delight, attacked the villagers' donkeys and began to plunder the fruit. The acrobats took advantage of the opportunity and set up shop in a broad open corner of the lane so that they could accomplish something before it got late and the people went to their houses.

7

I was born in a black tent. On the day of my birth they kept a mare away from her nursing colt so she would neigh. In those days the djinn and devils were terrified of a horse's neighing. The moment I was born and it was known that, thank God, I was a boy and not a girl, my father shot a rifle into the air. I began life in a tent with rifle shots and a horse's neighing.

At the age of four I sat behind a saddle horn. It wasn't long before they put a light rifle into my hands. Until the age of ten I had not spent even one night in a town or a house in a town.

Our tribe passed near Shiraz twice a year. Peddlers and hawkers from the city would spread carpets of sweets and helva along the path of the tribe. There was little cash money. I would get wool and dried curds from my relatives and give myself a treat. I can still taste those wind-swept, rained-on, dust-covered sweets.

I would jump for joy at the mention of the word "city," and when my father and later my mother were exiled to Tehran, I was the only member of the family who was happy. I didn't know they would take my horse and saddle away and seat me behind a desk and bench. I didn't know they would take my pretty practice rifle away and put a pen in my hand.

My father was not an important man. He was exiled by mistake. My mother was not an important woman either. She too was exiled by mistake. Everything we possessed was pillaged by government officials, also by mistake.

The period of our exile was fraught with difficulty and lasted more than eleven years. We were on the verge of going out into the lanes and begging. Agents of the police kept watch over us lest we beg. No news ever came of our belongings and property. Expenses had us by the throat. In the beginning we had a maid and a manservant, but as soon as the two of them saw a change for the worse in store, they fled and entrusted us to God.

For people who were used to unfurling their tents next to the most limpid springs, the water from the Tehran cisterns of those days was a catastrophe. For people who were accustomed to the fire of yew and chestnut, charcoal in a brazier and kerosene in a heater were calamities. For people whose galloping fields were beautiful and vast Fars, life in a narrow, dusty lane meant death and non-existence. For my mother, who had spent her entire life in an open, airy tribal tent, it was difficult and debilitating to breathe in a confined little room. We pitched a tent for her in the courtyard, and it was only the killing cold and snow of winter that could draw her into the four walls of the room.

8

A splendid gold dome appeared along with its beautiful minarets, and another, a blue dome, twin to the first, appeared, which was like an inappropriate patch in the midst of the mud houses.

It was nearly dusk when the caravan entered an avenue, on both sides of which were broken-down walls and small shops. Here there arose a dreadful clamor: impudent Arabs, stupid faces with fezzes on their heads, sly countenances beturbaned, with hennaed beards and fingernails and shaven heads. They twirled rosary beads and walked in sandals, cloaks, and long drawers. They were speaking in Persian, or they were gobbling in Turkish, or Arabic was emerging from the depths of their throats and from within their bowels and resonating in the air. Arab women with filthy tattooed faces and bleary eyes had rings through their nostrils. One of them had shoved her black breast half way down the throat of a dirty child she had in her lap.

This crowd of people was attracting customers by various means: one wailed, one beat his breast, one sold blessed seals, rosaries, and shrouds, one exorcised demons, one wrote prayers, and one rented out houses.

Long-cloaked Jews were buying gold and jewels from the travelers. In front of a coffee-house an Arab was sitting, one finger in his nose, and with his other hand he was picking the filth from between his toes. His face was covered with flies, and lice crawled up his head.

When the caravan stopped, Mashdi Ramazan and Hossein Aqa ran forward and helped get Khanom Galin and Aziz-Aqa out of the litter. A large crown attacked the travelers. Every piece of their luggage was in the hands of a different person, and they were inviting them to their houses. However, in the midst of this Aziz-Aqa got lost. No matter how hard they looked for her, no matter whom they asked, it was useless.

Finally, after Khanom Galin, Hossein Aqa, and Mashdi Ramazan had rented a dirty mud room at the rate of seven rupees a night, they set out again in search of Aziz-Aqa. They went around the entire city. They asked the shoe-keeper and the clerics one by one about Aziz-Aqa by name and description. There was no trace of her. It was late in the day. The courtyard had emptied out somewhat. Khanom Galin entered the sanctuary for the ninth time and saw a group of women and clerics gathered around a woman who was clinging to the lock of the grate, kissing it, and crying out.

However much they asked her what had happened, she would not answer. Finally, after much insistence, she said, "I have done something. I'm afraid the Lord of Martyrs will not forgive me."

She kept repeating this phrase, and a flood of tears sprang from her eyes. Khanom Galin recognized Aziz-Aqa's voice. She went forward, took her by the hand, and led her into the courtyard. With Hossein Aqa's help they took her to the house and gathered around her. After they gave her two sweet teas and got a waterpipe going for her, Aziz-Aqa stipulated that Hossein Aqa should leave the room so she could tell her story. When Hossein Aqa had gone out, Aziz-Aqa drew the waterpipe to herself and began thus.

Reading Selections (Classical)

1

In a city a tailor had a shop at the city gate by the graveyard, and he had hung a jug on a nail, and it was his passion to throw a stone into the jug for every funeral procession that was taken through the city gate, and every month he would count the stones to see how many people had been carried out. Then he would empty the jug and begin throwing stones in again. This continued for a long time, and then the tailor too died. A man came in search of the tailor, not knowing of his death. He saw the shop door closed. He asked [the tailor's] neighbor, "Where is the tailor. He's not here." The neighbor said, "The tailor too fell into the jug."

2

They say one day Anosharvan the Just was out hunting with his elite courtiers and passed by a village. He saw an old man ninety years old planting a walnut in the ground. Anosharvan was astonished because it takes twenty years for a planted walnut to bear fruit. "Old man," he said, "are you planting walnuts?"

"Yes, lord," he said.

"Do you think you'll live long enough to eat its fruit?" he asked.

The old man said, "[Others] planted and we eat, so we plant that [others] may eat."

Anosharvan was pleased. "Bravo!" he said. Immediately he told the treasurer to give the old man a thousand drachmas.

The old man said, "O lord, no one has eaten the fruit of this walnut sooner than your servant."

"How so?" he asked.

The old man said, "If I had not been planting walnuts and your majesty had not been passing by here, what came to me would not have come, and had your servants not given that answer, where would I have gotten a thousand drachmas from?"

Anosharvan said, "Bravo! Bravo!" The treasurer at once gave him another two thousand drachmas because 'bravo' had twice crossed Anosharvan's tongue.

3

It has been related that there was a petty merchant, and he wanted to go on a trip. He had a hundred maunds of iron. He placed it on deposit in the house of a friend and departed. When he came back, the trustee had sold the deposit and spent the proceeds. One day the merchant went to him to ask for his iron. The man said, "I had put your iron in a pit in the house and taken all precaution. There was a mouse hole there. By the time I realized it, it had eaten it all."

The merchant replied, "You're right. Mice love iron a lot, and their teeth are capable of gnawing iron."

The "honest" trustee became happy, that is he thought the merchant had grown soft and given up hope of the iron. He said, "Be a guest in my house today."

"I'll come back tomorrow," he replied. He departed, and when he reached the head of the lane he carried off one of the man's sons and hid him. When they sought for him and heralded throughout the city, the merchant said, "I saw a hawk carrying off a boy."

The trustee shouted, saying, "Why do you say lies and such absurd things? How can a hawk pick up a child?"

The merchant laughed and said, "In a city where a mouse can eat a hundred maunds of iron, a hawk can pick up a child of ten maunds."

The trustee realized what was going on. He said, "Mice did not eat the iron. Give me my son back and take your iron."

4

Anecdote

I heard of a king who indicated that a prisoner should be killed. The poor fellow, in that state of hopelessness, began to curse and revile the king, for they have said that he who gives up hope of life will blurt out whatever is on his mind.

At the time of necessity, when no escape remains, the hand will grab the tip of a sharp sword.

When man despairs his tongue grows long, like a cornered cat attacking a dog.

The king asked, "What is he saying?" One of the viziers of good counsel said, "O lord, he says, 'And those who bridle their anger and forgive people.' " The king had mercy and spared his life.

The other vizier, who was the opposite of the other, said, "It is not appropriate that people like us say anything other than the truth in the presence of kings. This man cursed the king and spoke inappropriately."

The king frowned at these words and said, "That lie of his was more pleasing to me than this truth you have spoken because the former was based on prudent action, but the latter was based in vileness." The wise have said, "A prudent lie is better than a seditious truth."

It would be a pity for anyone upon whose words the king acts to say anything other than what is good.

On Freidoun's arch was written:

The world, O brother, does not remain for anyone. Bind your heart to the creator of the world, and that is enough.

Do not rely on the kingdom of this world, for it has nourished and then killed many like you.

When a pure soul is about to depart, what difference does it make whether to die on a throne or in the dust?

Anecdote

One of the kings of Khurasan saw Mahmud son of Sabuktegin in a dream a hundred years after his death, when his entire body had disintegrated and turned to dust—except for his eyes, which kept on turning in their sockets and looking around. All the wise men failed to interpret this, but a dervish who made an obeisance said, "He is still worried because his kingdom is with others."

Many a renowned person has been buried under the ground, of whose existence upon the earth no trace remains.

And that old carrion they entrusted to the clay has been so gobbled up by the earth that not even the bones remain.

Alive is the splendid name of Anosharvan for justice, although much time has passed

41

since his sweet soul ceased to exist.
Do good, O so-and-so, and make the most of life before the cry goes up that so-and-so
is no more.

5

Melancholia is a malady in the treatment of which physicians have failed. Although melancholic illnesses are all chronic, melancholia has the characteristic of taking a long time to go away. In the book *Hippocratic Treatment*—a book on medicine the likes of which no one has ever made—Abu'l-Hasan b. Yahya has enumerated how many *imams*, doctors, learned men, and philosophers were afflicted with this malady.

My master told me that one of the House of Buya developed melancholia, and in this malady it seemed to him that he was a cow. All day long he bleated and said to one or another, "Kill me, for my meat will make good porridge." Things got so bad that he would not eat anything, and as time went on he was wasting away. The physicians were incapable of treating him.

During this time Avicenna was vizier, and the king, Ala'oddawla Mohammad b. Doshmanziar, held him in high esteem and had placed the entire kingdom in his hands and left all administration to his management. In truth, after Alexander, whose vizier was Aristotle, no king had ever had a vizier like Avicenna. While Avicenna was vizier, he would rise every day before dawn and compose two pages of the *Ketâb-e Shefâ*. When true dawn broke he would give audience to his students—like Kia Ra'is Bamanyar, Abu-Mansur b. Zila, Abdol-Wahed Juzjani, Solayman Dameshqi, and me, Bakalijar.

Until mid-morning we would read our lessons and then follow him in prayer, and by the time we came out there would be a thousand mounted persons from among the famous and nobles, people in need, and petitioners gathered around the gate of his house. The *khwaja* would mount, and that group would go with him. By the time he reached the divan, those mounted would have become two thousand. Then he would stay in the divan until the midday prayer, and when he returned [home], he would come to the dinner table. A group of people would eat with him. Then he would occupy himself with a nap, and when he arose he would pray and go to the king. There was deliberation and discussion with him until the afternoon prayer. In running the affairs of the kingdom there were just the two of them and never a third person. The purport of this story is that the *khwaja* had no leisure.

Then, when the physicians were incapable of treating that young man, they spoke of the situation to the great king of kings, Ala'oddawla, and persuaded him to intercede and tell Avicenna to treat the young man. Ala'oddawla so indicated, and Avicenna accepted. Then he said, "Give that young man the good news that the butcher is coming to kill him." They told the young man. He rejoiced. Then the *khwaja* mounted and went with his retinue to the gate of the patient's house. He entered along with one or two people, picked up a knife, and said, "Where's the cow so I can kill him?"

The young man mooed like a cow, as though to say, "He's here." The *khwaja* said, "Bring him into the middle of the house, bind his hands and feet, and throw him down."

When the patient heard this, he ran to the middle of the house and lay on his right side, and they bound his feet tightly. Then Avicenna came forth, rubbed one knife against the other, sat down, and put his hand on [the young man's] side, as is the custom of butchers. Then he said, "Oh! What a skinny cow this is! This one is not worth killing. Give him fodder so he'll get fat." He arose, went out, and told the people, "Unbind his hands and feet, put before him the food I order, and tell him to eat to get fat."

They did as the *khwaja* ordered. They brought him food, and he ate. After that they gave him all the potions and medicine [Avicenna] ordered and said, "Eat well, for it will fatten up this cow well." He heard and ate in hopes that he would get fat enough to be killed.

Then the physicians began to treat him as Avicenna ordered. Within a month he was cured and recovered, and all the people of wisdom know that such treatment cannot be done without perfect learning, complete knowledge, and a correct guess.

Lightning Source UK Ltd.
Milton Keynes UK
UKHW010810250121
377629UK00002B/268